Recapture

ANN—
I pray God will
use the words of this book
to Recapture your heart

Finding Hope During a Famine of the Heart

Recapture

Becky White

TRUSTED
BOOKS
A DIVISION OF DEEP RIVER BOOKS

Unless otherwise indicated, all Scriptures are taken from the *Holy Bible, New International Version, NIV®*. Copyright © 1973, 1978, 1984 International Bible Society. Used by permission of Zondervan Bible Publishers.

Scripture references marked MSG are taken from *The Message* Copyright © 1993. Used by permission of NavPress Publishing Group.

Hard Cover:
ISBN 13: 978-1-63269-091-3

Soft Cover:
ISBN 13: 978-1-63269-102-6

Library of Congress Catalog Card Number: 2008910942

Dedicated to my boys,
Trevor, Logan,
Boone, and Cameron:
My four most amazing gifts from God.
I love you.

Contents

Acknowledgments ix

Introduction: A Desperate Woman xiii

PART I: THE FAMINE

PART II: THE HARVEST

Acknowledgments

A MERE "THANK you" seems hardly adequate to express the feeling in my heart toward all the people who have made this book possible. Yet I pray that God will cause these two simple words to convey the deep gratitude I feel for each of them.

To all the women who have sat across from me at my desk or whom I have met in a crowded restaurant or even in the aisle of a store, and who have discovered truths about life, famine, and hope with me, thank you. To Tom and Carol and The Grove for opening a door for me to do ministry, thank you. To the women of my Bible Study who have encouraged my heart every week as we shared truth from God's word, thank you.

To the army of volunteers who made this challenging year of transition possible led by Clark and Diane, Nancy, Kevin, Ade, Marianne, Pastor Jim, Rose, Joe and Diane, Sande, and Teresa, thank you.

To those who have lovingly cared for Cameron over these many years to allow our family to be encouraged and thrive, Dr. Metsch, Dr. Ashwal, Susan, Cathy, Maria, Laurie, and Shirley and her amazing family at Rainbow House, Thank You from the depths of my heart.

To my friends who have spent countless hours reading this manuscript cover to cover, thank you. To April who has opened a way to communicate over the internet the heart and desire of this book, thank you. To Mary, whose creativity with design vividly brought the words on the cover to life, thank you. To Kevin, whose eye behind a camera caught a great picture of my family in a dry, open field, thank you. To my editors, Joe, Viv, Kim, Vesta, Christal, and Michelle, who lovingly used their red pens to help me clarify and re-shape my thoughts, thank you. To Veola, who from the first word encouraged me to paint a picture of our lives that would make the truths I explored in this book come to life, thank you. To Pat, whose work and tireless effort made it possible for this book to be published, thank you. To my friends who have graciously allowed me to share their stories with those who read these pages, thank you.

Words cannot begin to express my gratitude to Dr. Wallace Bratt, who from the moment he saw the early stages of this manuscript, never dropped it as he constantly encouraged me, telling me that I had a voice that needed to be heard. Thank you for helping me refine and clarify that voice, for lovingly and patiently looking at each sentence to bring order to the passions and overflow of my heart. This book would not have reached a shelf without you. Thank you, Wally. To my friend Sandy, who over the past ten years has listened to my account of each of the events that broke my heart as well as to those that brought me hope, thank you for championing the dream of writing this book and on many days for keeping the flame alive. To my Mom and Dad, and my sisters and their husbands, whose unending love and support made this book possible, thank you. To my guys, who have lived beside me as these stories changed all of our lives, I cannot begin to tell each of you how proud I am of you and the young men you are becoming. Thank you for struggling with me through the challenges, for embracing our joy to the fullest measure, and most of all, for allowing me to open the doors of our home and share with others the amazing God we have met inside its walls throughout our deepest and darkest moments, as well as in the crazy, insane times that have made our life so rich. Being your Mom is the greatest joy of my life, and I thank you.

And finally, I pray that the words of this book will be poured out as an offering of gratitude to my God, whom I have worshiped since I was a little girl. I have learned that the worship You most love comes from the deepest and most raw parts of my heart. And it is from the depths of that place that the words of this book emanate, each one an offering to You. I thank You for withholding nothing in Your relentless effort to recapture my heart.

Introduction:

A Desperate Woman

~⚬⚬⚬~

IMAGINE YOURSELF IN a crowded house in the coastal city of Tyre, the part of the world we now call Lebanon. A strange, intriguing teacher has come north from his native Israel. Everywhere He goes He has created such a stir that He is always followed by large crowds.

He has become famous for healing people with diseases of all kinds. Even those who are possessed by evil spirits come to Him and find total healing. You are drawn in and possibly even have something you hope He can fix. Maybe you have a need bigger than you and wonder, *Maybe this Jesus can make me whole.* So you join the crowd and wait your turn in a noisy house buzzing with wonder about this fascinating young man.

When He walks into the house, He seems no different than anyone else. The men with Him, too, are not extraordinary, but very normal. Many of them look like the rough, strong fishermen you have seen all your life in the city of Tyre. But after closer inspection, there is something different about them. They seem to possess a look of wonder and awe as they watch the Man they follow.

When the Teacher walks quietly into the room, many people press in to get close to Him. You stay back, uncertain. You are sure that in a crowd this size He would never have the time or the inclination to deal with your problem.

Suddenly a woman bursts into the crowded, now stuffy house. She is yelling. She is desperate. She looks to be about your age, but the lines on her dark skin add years to her intense face. She shouts frantically for the attention of the Teacher. She calls Him the "son of David"[1] and she begs for mercy. The mercy she desires is not for her; no, her pleas are for another person who is suffering. She is a mother and her child is very sick. Crowded against the wall of the house, you feel a strong sense of pity for the woman, and you watch anxiously to see if this young Teacher can do anything to help her. Will He reach beyond the walls of this dwelling, beyond the current cultural and physical barriers to heal an innocent child who is suffering?

You can see the desperation etched into the face of this young mother. You can hear it in her voice as it continues to rise above others until she is heard. And yes, she is heard—by everyone in the house. But the One she is addressing does not speak to her. His disciples answer her instead. The strong and rugged men who followed the Teacher into the room are the first to respond to her cries. You wait and hope they will have something for her, some kind of hope. But instead of helping her, instead of becoming her advocate, they go to Jesus and urge Him to send her away. Her suffering, her cries are embarrassing to them. She is loud and she makes them feel uncomfortable. Besides, she is a foreigner. She is not from Israel. You are not from Israel either and, as a matter of fact, neither are most of the others standing around in the crowded house that night.

The answer of the young Teacher silences all who are taking in the scene. He simply says He has come to give to the "lost sheep of *Israel.*"[2] You think the woman will be stunned and angry. You expect her to turn and walk away, but she does not. She continues to press in toward Him, looks Him in the eye, and falls at His feet. Even after He says things that would seem to discourage any hope she had, she continues to plead with Him. He is all she has left, her only hope. Deep within her she knows He has the power to heal her daughter, and she is certain that power is available to her.

You watch the scene unfold with shock and amazement. She is right about Jesus. He bends down and lifts her up off the dirt floor. He gently wipes her tears and looks straight into her eyes. He tells her that at that very moment her daughter is healed. It is her faith that brought the healing. The room becomes silent and the woman turns and walks out with her head held high. Because her Lord, the Creator and the Savior of the world, has not only healed her daughter; He has recaptured her heart. He has allowed her to know great suffering, but in His amazing grace He has brought that suffering to an end. She came passionately seeking the only One who could give her hope, the only One who could heal her daughter, the only One who could make her whole. She would not take "no" for an answer. She knew it was her right, her privilege, and even her mandate to ask Him to make the wrong thing in her life right.

You, the witness to this encounter, leave the house that night without ever talking to Him. You never even asked Him to fix what was wrong with you. You can't even remember what it was. All you can think of is the woman's face, and you hear her voice over and over in your head. You long for that kind of passion. Because, just like that woman, you have known pain, struggle, and desperation. You want to be able to come to Him in that way. You want determination so strong that you will not be pushed aside or ignored. You don't care who sees you, what you have to do, or where you have to go. You are convinced you deserve to be whole. At that moment, you would have done anything to have the kind of courage that woman showed. It is the kind of courage that lands you at the feet of your Redeemer.

Have you ever been that desperate woman? Have you ever been one who could care less about what others think of you? This woman had a single focus, tunnel vision, and she could think of only one thing. She was totally consumed with taking her burden to the only One who could carry it for her.

If you have been her, you will never forget that moment when He lifted you from the ground and exchanged your exhausted cries for tears of joy. Have you ever had your heart recaptured?

Listen to these words spoken by God to some pretty desperate people. "I will do *this* to recapture the hearts of the people."[3] (italics mine) What God does in our lives to recapture us shows that we belong to Him. The word recapture not only implies intent; it also implies ownership. He has no intention of allowing us to miss what life lived in abundance here on earth can hold for us. But as we live that life, we would like to tell Him that there are parts we can do without. We tell Him that what He does to "recapture" us at times feels like it is destroying us—loss, death, famine, disease. We feel robbed, hopeless, and even helpless to live this life because it feels impossible.

On many days we only fear we don't have enough to carry on, and on other days we are sure of it. We know we don't have enough strength, joy, endurance, or even enough will to do what that desperate woman did—to push through the pain. But we must endure the pain because He wants our hearts. In order for us to give Him that fallen, deceitful organ full of all kinds of desires, it must first go through a process of breaking, squeezing, and rending. Like the desperate woman, those who have experienced this process can walk out of the presence of their Creator with their heads held high, wiping away dirt-stained tears and exhausted from the process. But they are also victorious, and they have a story to tell. Can you imagine how many heard from that woman about her encounter with Jesus? When we meet God in those desperate, intense, life-altering moments and find Him to be enough, we too will have a story to tell. And we have a captive audience, for there is a world in famine waiting for the answer to one question, "Where is the food?" You can tell them it is at the feet of your Redeemer.

That is where we find Ruth as we look at her story. The ancient tale of Ruth and mother-in-law Naomi has a message that is crying to be heard. It has a message of hope in the face of unspeakable loss, of new life in the face of death, and of food in the midst of famine. These women cared for all the same kinds of things we care about today. They loved their families, they harbored hopes and dreams, they had fears and they had famines. And most of all they found in their most desperate moments a God who could redeem it all. As you read the pages of *Recapture*, I pray you will find God in the famines of your life. And more than that, I pray you will have the courage, determination, and even desperation to fall at His feet and let Him recapture your heart.

Part I

The Famine

Chapter One

Famine

In the days when the judges ruled there was a famine in the land, and a man from Bethlehem in Judah, together with his wife and two sons, went to live for a while in the country of Moab. The man's name was Elimelech, his wife's name Naomi, and the names of his two sons were Mahlon and Kilion. They were Ephrathites from Bethlehem, Judah. And they went to Moab and lived there.[1]

WHAT COMES TO mind when you hear the word "famine?" Do you think of a dry desert town in the middle of central Africa? Hundreds of thousands dying in filth in villages? Or maybe you think of a child living in poverty without enough to eat. Is what you think of dry? Desolate? Depressing? Far away? Chances are that, like me, you have never been a part of that kind of famine. But that does not mean our lives do not have famines. Let's take a few minutes to expand our understanding of how we define the word "famine."

Certainly it includes the dry town and the hungry child, but famine is much more than that. What if we thought of it as anything we were created to need but do not have? With that definition in mind, the possibilities of famine can include the physical kind we mentioned. But it could also include emotional, relational, and spiritual famines. It is not a lack of something we merely want, like a newer car, a bigger house, or a different reflection in the mirror. A famine is when we have a deficit, a space between what we really need and what we have. That space can be huge. There can be a widening gap between what our body, mind, and heart are crying out for and the reality of what our life actually contains. That famine, deficit, or gap can last for a period of time, a season. But some famines might just last for the rest of our lives. We may never have what we were created to need, and the realization of that can drive us to the end of ourselves and keep us in a place of helplessness and total dependence. And that is exactly where I want to begin.

That is where we find Naomi and Ruth. They lived centuries ago, but their story of courage and hope in the face of heart-wrenching despair speaks honest, rich, deep truth into our complex famines of today. They are the two central figures in this ancient book that we will look at together. They are at the end of themselves. They are in the midst of famine.

As we walk with them through their journeys, we will see not only how God met them in their famines, but even more, how He recaptured their hearts. That word "recapture" is used most often in our day to refer to the act of marking an animal and sending it out into the wild only to be captured again. I love that picture. That is exactly what God does in our lives as we live in famines, as we experience death, loss, grief, and bitterness. All of those profound things will be used powerfully by God to recapture our hearts.

Just like Ruth and Naomi, our famines can take us to the edge, to the end of ourselves, to that place of fear, almost of panic, where we hear words like: "It looks like cancer," "I want a divorce; I never loved you," "There is not a cure, no hope, no option, nothing else we can do." It is those kinds of words that create instant famines in our lives. And it is our response to those words that defines our character, the character those events are forging in our lives.

Famine can come in many forms and is no respecter of persons. Famine can hit that child in the African village as well as the man living in a mansion. It is present in poverty of every form, and it is present in wealth beyond our imagination. The truth is, regardless of how much we have, if we do not possess what we were created to need, we are in a famine. And we have one burning question, "Where is the food?"

IN THE BAG

One Saturday morning not long ago, I went to McDonald's at the request of my sons Logan and Boone, two of my four boys. Trevor, my oldest, is 19 and I have 14-year-old triplets, Logan, Boone, and Cameron. Can you believe it? Even if I were sitting with you reading that short sentence, I still would not believe it. Four teenage boys! Triplets! No wonder I am asking where the food is!

I am crazy about my guys. They are my heart and the absolute joy of my life, but on that particular day they were not very happy with me. I had spent the week trying to eat healthier, and they felt like they were being punished. They had been craving their fast food, so I told them to wait until the weekend.

When Saturday morning came, I found myself at our old favorite place - the McDonald's I used to jog to, pushing my boys in their specially made triple stroller. As I drove up to the restaurant that day, however, I was painfully aware that I could no longer easily jog the two miles there on my own, let alone push a stroller with three little boys.

The last ten years of life had taken a toll on me. I no longer had the energy I used to have. I no longer had the drive, the determination, or even the youthful muscular athletic build I once had. I had a few more gray hairs, a lot more wrinkles, a few more bills, and a few more pounds. I was in a famine.

My son Cameron had been diagnosed with severe autism and retardation when he was still a toddler in that stroller, and now he was no longer small. In fact, the challenges of caring for Cam as a young teenager had grown faster than he had. And I was facing them alone because I was now a single mom. I had good reason to eat healthy that day. In fact, I was under doctor's orders to "make some changes" when I was recently discharged from a short stay in the hospital brought on by exhaustion and stress.

I was limited in time that morning, and as I drove into the parking lot I could see the drive-thru was packed, so I parked my car and walked inside.

As I entered, a nicely-dressed, distinguished-looking older man had just finished ordering in front of me. Also in the waiting area where I got my drinks was a very disheveled, homeless man who had been on the streets for what appeared to be a very long time. I waited for my order, took my food, and left in silence, still deep in my own thoughts.

As I walked across the parking lot toward my car, the older man passed me at a brisk pace. He made his way to the back of his van and took something out. He took off across the parking lot almost at a run as he waved and yelled at someone. I thought he was meeting friends for breakfast, but then I noticed he did not have his McDonald's bag; he was holding a plastic bag full of groceries he had taken from his mini-van. He was chasing the homeless man.

They met up across the shopping center and I watched from my car, thankful for the diversion from my own thoughts. The two men spoke briefly, and the homeless man walked away, leaving the older man still holding the bag. The man gestured that he would just leave the bag by the post where they were standing. However, he was quickly discouraged from that idea as the homeless man made it very evident he wanted no part of it by turning his back and waving his arm away.

I watched as the older man, the bag still in his hand, walked slowly back to his van, opened the hatchback, and placed the bag back inside. I looked to see if he had a car full of groceries, but the van was empty except for the single bag that he obviously had prepared for an opportunity like this. He closed the back of his van and went back into McDonald's to finish his breakfast.

I was not finished with my little observation, though. In fact, I became Becky the stalker. I had been pulled into this little drama and I wanted to get the full picture. I drove away in the direction the homeless man was walking. He was now across the parking lot in front of the grocery store. As I got closer to him, I watched as he went from car to car begging for change.

I drove away, hit my blinker, and turned out of the parking lot toward home, shaking my head. But before I could even begin to form a thought about the choices this man had made, God quickly spoke to my heart. *Becky, that is exactly what you do to me. I am the man holding the bag, and you are that homeless person in need, in the middle of famine. I come to you with a bag full of everything you need to endure the famine, and you turn and walk away from me to go and beg someone else to give it to you.*

Wow, talk about conviction! What a drag of a way to start a Saturday morning. I liked it better when I was lost in my depressed musing of the past. But in those moments of watching the homeless man, God pulled me vividly, painfully, and truthfully to the present. And He showed me I had not only walked away from food in the middle of my famine; I had walked away from Him.

In a sense, I was not far from Him. In fact, I had just been talking to Him during the week, right after a particularly disturbing doctor's appointment. Actually, I had been talking to Him very loudly and passionately. I had cried out to Him. I had yelled at Him. I remember telling Him in a not-so-worshipful, sarcastic tone that was even a tad condemning, "God, do you know what is wrong with famine? There is no food. People die in the famine because there is nothing to eat. God, I am not leaving this famine, I am enduring it. But I am dying without the food. Where is the food?"

On my way home from McDonald's that morning with God's words still bouncing around in the silence of my brain, I began to laugh at the simplicity and clarity of it all. Here was this nice, kind, friendly old man who just appeared in my life. He was holding a plastic grocery sack out to a man obviously in the midst of famine. And what did the grocery bag contain? Food.

You know how you have those moments when you are sure that as the light bulb goes on in your mind, God leans forward with His angels in anticipation that finally this poor, slow-minded woman has grasped truth. Can't you see them? Sort of like a bunch of guys around a television set transfixed in eager anticipation to see if their team will finally score a touchdown.

As the truth washes over me, I nod my head in understanding, and I picture Him sitting back after a long exhale, high-fiving those angels and saying, "Finally, I think she might just make it, guys." I will make it, but it sure is not easy. It is a lot tougher to live out this life than I thought. But I am going to do it. And somehow along the way I will be able to not only find the food, but to share with others what that looks like, feels like, and tastes like. Maybe even with you.

Maybe you are in a famine. Maybe you have just spent the day wondering where you will find the food. I will tell you where it is. Not at McDonald's – although I must say the food is pretty tasty there. No, you find the food in the hand of the One who prepared it just for you. God is holding the food, and He is chasing you down today.

What is in that bag for you? That bag is full of riches: love, worth, value, purpose, and promises beyond our wildest dreams. Everything we need in the famine and everything He needs to recapture our hearts is in that bag. But many days, in our obviously desperate state, we leave Him holding the bag as we go from person to person, begging them to give us even a portion of what they have. It is our fear that drives us away - like Elimilech's family in the story of Ruth - to Moab, to someone, to anyone we can beg to give us food. And it is that same fear that fuels our pride to say at times that we don't need the bag. It causes us to wave God off when He tries to leave the bag on the curb for us.

What has caused your famine today? And what is driving you to walk away from the One with the bag? Has it been your own choice causing shame and guilt so great you cannot even look at Him, let alone take something out of that bag? Or maybe you once took a bag full of dreams from the hand of someone else, someone you trusted, and you were left not only empty and devastated, but the choice of that person actually brought you the famine you now endure.

Perhaps you looked in the bag God is holding out to you. Maybe your problem today is that your famine came from the bag He holds. Like the challenges brought into my life through my son Cameron, your famine first touched the hand of God before He gently allowed it into your life, and now you want no part of what else that bag might contain. Regardless of where the famine came from, you have a choice of how to respond when the needs of your heart explode into a reality you never expected.

So, if famine is the lack of something you were created to need, what is the solution? How do you take hold of the food? What can make you turn from the person you are begging from and walk back to the man holding the bag? What is your famine today? What will you do in the face of that widening gap between need and reality? We have several choices, choices that affect us and others in life-altering ways.

The first choice is to try to escape the famine. We can go to the next person we see getting into a car and beg for something, anything to take this pain away. Escape could be as simple as trying to meet that need in your heart by going to the fridge or the mall, or as devastating as going to a person, the wrong person, to try to fill that gaping hole in your heart.

Another option is to stick it out, to stay in the famine. Instead of acknowledging the gap, instead of feeling the pain and loss famine brings, we simply control our famine. We decide what our heart is allowed to feel, and suddenly the famine is gone. But is it really? Or have we simply waved off the food and let the parts of our heart die that were created to need those things?

The final option is to endure the famine with all our desires and needs intact. We can choose to have the courage to face the places where we have not only a little gap, but a gaping hole. And we can choose to not only know it's there, but to feel it each and every day of our lives. In fact, we can feel it so deeply and profoundly that it drives us daily to God to find what is in the bag for us. We have the freedom to blurt out that one question as we fall at His feet, the question that comes out most often in a flood of tears. In anger, confusion, and even some condemnation we ask Him, "Where is the food?"

Will you begin to listen to Him today as He reaches down and whispers in your ear, "It's in the bag"?

FAMINE IN RUTH

Imagine for a few minutes what life was like for Elimelech. His story unfolds as the book of Ruth opens. He is the husband of Naomi and the father of two sons. Every day this farmer walked out of his little home to see his crops. And each day he saw those plants shrivel up and bend until they returned to the ground he had planted them in. Each morning as he walked, his fields dry from the lack of rain, he must have thought long and hard about what to do. Elimelech was living in a famine. There was no rain, no food, no water, nothing was green. Every day as he walked, all he could see were the brown fields. All was silent except for the sound of dry stalks snapping as he took each step.

How many days did he kick the dust of the field before he raised his eyes to see the only green that was visible, the fertile hills of the neighboring country to the north, Moab? For days he walked that field, coming into his house to face his wife Naomi and two sons empty-handed. Elimelech had not been alive to experience some of the most amazing events in the history of the nation of Israel. He had not seen the plagues in Egypt. He had not been one of the million people who crossed not only a desert but the Red Sea on the way to their "Promised Land." Perhaps as a boy he had heard stories of these miracles of God's deliverance, but he had not seen them with his own eyes. He was simply a farmer, like many other men in Bethlehem.

The period Elimelech lived through was one of the most tumultuous eras in Israel's history. There was no king in Israel; instead, Judges ruled the nation. These years without a king were described as a time when "everyone did as he saw fit."[2]

So as Elimelech walked the fields each day, feeling the reality of his hunger, what he saw fit to do was to escape. He saw the green hills of Moab, he felt the need in his belly as it groaned for lack of food, and he thought of his wife and boys. Finally the gap got too wide, the need too great, and he made a decision. He chose to close the gap, to fix the problem, to escape the famine; he took his small family to Moab.

So what is the big deal? What is wrong with going to Moab? It makes perfect sense to us that if what you need is not provided where you live, you get in your car and drive to where you can find it. But that is not how it worked in Israel. God had promised the people this certain piece of land; it was their inheritance. He promised He would provide for them there. That means if you don't have what you need, you stay put until God gives it to you. There are lots of stories about famine, and almost without exception the people were to stay in the land God promised them. The purpose of many of those times of famine was for the people to learn to trust God.

But Elimelech had not learned that trust firsthand. He had not actually watched the waves part and had not set his sandaled foot on dry land as his ancestors had when they crossed through the sea. He had not eaten the manna God sent from the sky as the nation of Israel wandered through the desert for 40 years. In fact, as he walked his dry fields he could not remember the last time anything fell from the sky. All he knew was that he and his family were in a famine. There was a huge, growing gap between what he was created to need and what he had. He did not trust God; he trusted only his own decisions, and unfortunately, this particular choice was not only wrong, it was tragic. The outcome of his choice to escape the famine was death, not only for himself, but also for his sons. We cannot escape famine; we must endure it.

OUR FAMINES

Are you in the middle of a famine today? As you read this do you feel the longing, churning, rumbling in your spirit for what you need, yet do not have? What is it for you? What has created the gap? Was it death, divorce, loneliness, loss of health, hopes, and dreams? What does it feel like for you each morning as you walk around on that dry, brittle ground of those hopes and dreams and come in again and again empty-handed, alone? May I ask you, in your place of loss have you allowed your eyes to wander to Moab, to the territory that looks green and promising? Do you say, "If only I had the right person in my life, the right job, the right parents, the right doctor, the right diagnosis, the right body, or the right friends"?

In those moments of famine, as we walk the dry, desert times of our lives, our hearts are saying, "If only I had someone who really understood that I simply cannot go another day without food!" But instead of going to the One who understands our famine, the One who even allowed it in our lives, we look elsewhere; we look at Moab.

Moab may be a different place for each of us. It can be summed up simply as going to the wrong place for the wrong things. The form Moab takes, however, can be complex and at times disastrous.

As I suggested earlier, going to Moab could be as simple as heading to the fridge, the pantry, the ice cream or donut shop when life goes a little wrong. It could be grabbing your credit card and hitting the mall or the internet to buy something "just because it will feel good to wear something new." Will it really feel good? If you are in Moab, by the time the new shirt you ordered arrives, you probably have already had too many trips to the fridge for it to fit anyway. It's a defeating cycle.

Those things are discouraging, but there are even more defeating choices we can make to try to escape famine. Going to Moab can also include trying to have your needs met by another job, another house, or another person. I can assure you wherever or whatever Moab is for you, it holds death. When we try to escape our famines, when we try to find food on our own, and when we run away from our problems, death awaits us. It may be death to our health, our waistline, our pocketbook, or it could be death to relationships, security, and safety. And do you know what else? The famine will just follow us there, because guess who is going to Moab with us? We are! As flawed as we allow ourselves to remain, we are simply running from every effort God is making to recapture our hearts.

We cannot run from our famines; they are the very tools God uses to refine us, strengthen us, and forge us into the people He had in mind when He made us. We cannot become that person God intended us to be in Moab, as we run from our problems and try to escape the needs in our hearts and lives. We become the person He created us to be in the middle of the famine. We become that person in the midst of need, desire, and loss. There certainly are moments, though, when we go to God and shake our heads and tell Him there is no way we can do this. We tell Him He can't possibly mean for us to go through this alone. Certainly He cannot expect us to even meet the needs of others when we have so few resources ourselves. We think God never intended us to feel this much pain. We think it must be wrong and there must be some other way.

I wish I could tell you why life has to hurt so much. I wish I could tell you why you have that hole in your heart, why there has to be a famine in your life. I can only tell you that if you will just stand there in the dry and empty field, God will show up. He will meet you there. He is not in Moab. He is in the dry, brittle places of our lives. He is not asking you to do anything. Most often there is little we can do to alter our famines. All He desires for you to do is just stand there and wait for Him.

I have been doing a lot of standing and waiting in dry and dusty fields over the last few years. During this time, I have learned that God not only sees you in the famine and meets you there, but that others are watching you, too. My oldest son Trevor and I had a talk about that very thing the month he graduated from high school. If you had asked me what I dreamed for him when he was born just over eighteen years before, I would have said all the normal things. I wanted him to be healthy and to grow up in a safe, loving, secure home. I wanted him to have a deep and personal relationship with God. I wanted him to be a man of integrity and character. And I believed at that time that all of that character would come from the environment of a calm home, free of major struggles. I never dreamed that his character would be formed through famine.

As I looked at my son that night, I could easily say he has surpassed any dream I had for him. He is tall, blonde, charming, and handsome beyond belief. He is a young man of integrity and character. As he was preparing to leave for college several states away, I was certain he was ready in every way possible for the challenges life would throw at him. Trevor has lived through the famine, and more than that, he has watched me live through it as well.

He and I had a great talk that evening. If on the day he was born I had written a script for him to read to me when he was eighteen, it would not have corresponded to the words that came out of his mouth. His own words were far more meaningful than my script would have been. As we talked, he told me that the things he had seen in me were the very things God had used to make him into the man he had become.

In our talk that lasted well over an hour, he never once mentioned a gift I had given him or a vacation we had taken. He never talked about the teams I had coached or the cupcakes I had baked. He only talked about the famines he had watched me endure. He talked about what he had learned from watching me raise him and his brothers as a single mom and what he had seen in the even greater challenges we faced with the disabilities of his brother Cameron. The two greatest famines in my life were the places God used to teach my son. I could not begin to tell you a single thing I did in those two overwhelming places in my life. All I have done is stand there. How in the world can you begin to tackle impossible places? There is no way. There is nothing you can do but wait, pray, hope, and keep standing.

"Flint" is not a term you hear very often, but it is the strongest surface imaginable. It is the exact word that describes how firm our direction must be. We have to "set our face like flint."[3] I have often asked God for that kind of determination to just have what I need to remain, stand, and survive. I wish I could give you a formula, I wish I could write out the steps for you or create a checklist. But that is not how survival in famine works. It is simply living each and every day with whatever it holds, from joy to heartbreak, from the ridiculous to the calm, from the impossible to the hilarious. My boys and I have experienced it all. And in the end, what all those days of famine add up to is character. When I see God doing that in my boys, when I see them grow into sensitive, loving, and caring young men, I realize I would not change things, even to make life easier. And the most shocking part for me is that God is actually using me! He is not making them into men of character in spite of me, but because of me! Now that is amazing! Only God could do that! Only God could recapture my heart and refine my boys at the same time.

So keep standing there. You don't have to like it. You don't have to fix it. You just have to trust that God is doing something you can't see, can't understand, and at times can't agree with. Your only choice is to just keep standing there. Just believe that as you do, He is recapturing your heart and others are watching. You may not know how it all works; you don't have to. Just stand there. Don't go to Moab, don't try to escape. Stay in the famine. Don't ignore it; don't close your heart to what it is begging for. Feel it.

Too often we are guilty of gutting out our famines by ourselves. We think that if we don't go to Moab, that is all that is required. We think that if we can grin and bear it or if we can just close off enough of our heart, our desires, our hopes, then maybe the groaning in our stomachs will stop. We can say things like "I really never wanted to have children" or "I am okay with this diagnosis; God can do whatever He wants." Really, are you okay with that? Are you really okay when God allows something in your life that creates a famine?

Well, I am not okay with that. I am pretty upset, actually. I am really mad, hurt, confused, and alone. When our life just plain stinks and there is not enough, why should we act like there is? Why should we smile when our hearts are breaking? Why do we go to God in prayer for the same old things every day while we completely ignore the searing pain in our hearts? Why aren't we honest with what we need? Why, when we walk the dry fields of our hearts and see the crops dying, do we come back into the house saying, "It's okay, no problem. I was not hungry anyway." Come on, you are starving and you know it!

What are you hungry for today? What have you said you do not need? What are you doing without but acting like you could care less? Is it love, a relationship, the child you could never have, or maybe it is the child you could never control? Are you without your health, your safety, your dreams, without order, or even without your hopes? When was the last time you went to God with what you were created to need in one hand and the truth of your life in the other and said, "What is this all about? I did not sign up for this life." I have done that, and I would like to tell you it felt great. Boy, did I ever give God a piece of my mind! Actually, what it felt like was honesty. It felt like worship. It felt like I finally put into words the feelings burning my heart.

Enduring famine in our lives has everything to do with courage. It is fear of failure that sends us to Moab, and it is fear of pain that makes us recoil and want to protect our hearts. And it is purely fear-driven pride that says, "We can do it. We can make it. I am strong enough, prepared enough, disciplined enough, obedient enough to make it through. And won't God be so proud of me when He sees what I did all by myself, without ever asking Him for help."

Boy, do we ever get that messed up! Whoever told us we could do it alone? Who told us it would be impressive to anyone, let alone God, that we made it through a famine without even a grimace?

Maybe you are shaking your head right about now, thinking you have never done that, but think again. You will not fool me! I have lived out a lifetime of famines with a smile on my face. I know how to do it, and I know it does not work. Because we all have famines, and if we try to survive famine with our own strength the result is resentment, bitterness, and a hard heart. There is a huge difference between strength and endurance. You will never make it through a famine on strength alone.

ENDURANCE FOR THE FAMINE

So we don't escape famines; we don't go to Moab. And we don't close up our hearts to what they need. But if we can't escape it and we have to feel it, how in the world do we survive it? How do you endure a famine? What does endurance look like? How does it help us in the midst of famine?

I was given the gift of looking at endurance close up, of watching someone endure a famine. It was quite a few years ago and I was struggling with a decision that had to be made. I was looking straight into one of those dreams that was dying, and I was stuck. I did not want to go to Moab. I wanted to stay in the famine, and I was trying to gut it out. I was acting like I didn't really care, like I didn't really need what I was losing anyway. But I was worn out from trying.

My triplets were little, in preschool at the time. My typical schedule was to bring Cameron, my special needs son, to his preschool. And then two days a week I drove my other two boys across town to their preschool. After dropping them off, I went home for an amazing quiet hour and then started the pickups. Those were, unfortunately, the most relaxing two days of my week. No wonder I was worn out.

On this particular day it was about noon and I had just picked up Cam from school and was driving across town to get Logan and Boone from their pre-school. My mind was filled with thoughts of the decision facing me. As I neared the boys' school I happened to notice a man in a wheelchair struggling on the sidewalk. As I drove past, God laid it on my heart to stop. I continued on my way. But I have had this happen before, and I was sure of what God wanted me to do. He wanted me to stop. So despite my schedule and all my internal arguments, I turned my minivan around and tried to find him. I parked and carried my four-year-old Cam back to the spot where I had seen the man. As I walked up to him, I noticed he had only gone a few feet from where I first saw him. I came up behind him and told him it appeared he was struggling, and I wondered if I could help him. As he turned, he gave me the most amazing and knowing smile. In that split second I knew I had not come to help him at all; it was very much the other way around.

He politely introduced himself to me and told me his name was Bryan. Bryan told me he had been in an accident that left him unable to walk, and it had also affected his speech. I introduced him to Cam and told him a little about Cam's disability as well. We talked together for just a few moments. As I was about to leave him, I remembered why I stopped in the first place and asked him if I could push him somewhere. He told me that was not necessary, because he was exercising.

I asked him, "Are you trying to get stronger, Bryan?"

He said, "No, it's about endurance."

I remember saying goodbye to him and turning to walk back toward my van. As I walked away I thought, *Wow, that stop was not at all for him, it was for me.* All my life it had been about strength, and when he said the word "exercise" I got it. I was an athlete; in fact I was a big-time athlete. I was an eight-time All American. I knew this stuff. I taught this stuff. I was all about exercise. *No matter the problem, the solution was always to be stronger,* I thought incorrectly. So, of course this poor man in the wheelchair would have to get stronger to endure this obvious famine. But Bryan had it right; he had learned volumes from his famine. He knew it had nothing to do with strength and everything to do with endurance.

As I walked back to the van carrying my tiny little boy, I had no idea of how the truth of Bryan's statement would resound in my head day after day. I had no idea of the famines that would be caused in my life by the extreme disabilities of my son. I did not know then that the strength I had worked so hard to cultivate all my life as an athlete would fail me as my body wore out, year after year. I did not know that the famines I was so certain I could make it through would leave me at times completely unable to function. I had no idea what famine was, and I did not know what endurance meant. But I do today.

I have learned it is all I have left. All I can do on most days is just keep moving, like Bryan, in the right direction. I have learned the endurance that you cultivate is all you need. Because it is when you endure that you find food in the famine. When you keep feeling, keep moving, keep that hope alive, and acknowledge your need, you will find you are not alone. God not only knows what you need and what you lack; He is prepared to meet you in that hot, parched field. And as He meets you there, He has no intention of giving you back what you lost, or even of giving you what you asked for. He plans to give you so much more.

JUST A BEGGAR

There was a man who lived in first century Jerusalem who knew all about famine, for he had endured it every day of his life. He had never escaped it; nor had he stopped feeling. In fact, he could do nothing else but feel and experience a life lived in deficit. So great was his famine that he was unable to even get himself to the spot at the temple gate relegated to him each day. He had to wait at his house for someone to carry him to the place where he sat and begged for something, anything to help with his famine. For years he endured the humility of being carried by other men to the dirty, smelly corner of the temple gate that was called, ironically, "beautiful."⁴ But one day was different from all the rest.

It probably started the same way as other days, with the jostled ride to his familiar spot. But in the middle of the afternoon he watched as two men approached. They must have looked like so many others who came through the temple. They were just two ordinary men, men who might provide him with just enough for the day's needs. As they approached, he asked the same thing he had asked a hundred times before, "Do you have any money to spare?" In other words, "I am not asking for much. Don't go out of your way for me. After all, I am not someone of importance, just a poor crippled man. So whatever you have extra will do. If you don't mind, will you just check and see if you have some spare change for me?" But the men he met that day were Peter and John, two of the disciples of Jesus, and on this day they wanted to give him much more than their spare change. They wanted to end his famine.

The first thing they did in this short yet profound encounter was to look straight at him. They saw him in his little corner of the world, in his famine. They saw him in his dry and desolate field. They took in the dirt, the smells, and the emptiness of his life. The second thing they did was ask for eye contact. You can just picture the man looking down in shame and embarrassment at the intent gaze the men had trained on him. After all, he was used to people just throwing him a few coins; never had they actually taken the time to notice what his world looked like. But these two men not only stopped; they asked him to look at them. So he lifted his eyes that held pain, hurt, loss, and disappointment, eyes that had little spark left in them. But behind his gaze was a heart that still held out the smallest amount of hope. He actually expected them to do something for him.

Peter's answer was clear and unbelievable. He had come to the man in his famine; he had listened to his request, acknowledged it, and then disregarded it in favor of something much better. Peter told him he would not give him silver or gold—no change for him. Instead, they told him to get up and walk. And that is exactly what he did. He stood up, and as the limp, lifeless muscles of his legs strengthened to hold his body, he began to dance and rejoice. His famine was over. He had come there as usual, hoping for just enough to make it through the day, and instead he was given a gift beyond his wildest dreams.

This is what God does for us as He comes to us in our famines. He does it in those places where we are determined to stay, feel, and be obedient. But as we walk, crawl, or are carried to that spot each day, we are at a loss as to what we can even ask for. So we simply ask for what we think we need. We ask for just some change, just enough to get us through the day. But when we come face to face with our Creator, He looks at us and He takes it all in. He sees the pain, the sorrow, the determination to stay in that place until He shows up. He not only looks at us, but He asks us to raise our tired, sad eyes to Him, truly expecting something. He wants us to stay in that need. He wants us to feel it because He wants to meet us there. He wants to give us more than we ask for, more than we could imagine. And He gives us what we truly need. He alone knows what it is.

There is such an amazing peace that comes over you when you experience God in the middle of your famine. He comes to us through people; He sends friends and family to strengthen and encourage us. And most of all, He comes to us Himself through His promises, the Bible, His very words, His truth. With those words He can end our famines. Or at times, with those words He comes to us and sits down beside us through the long nights, whispering the truth as we endure what seems impossible. Those words are the food we need to make it through the famine.

PROMISES

God's words have been the greatest source of food for the famines in my life. Each week as I have studied the Bible, He has given me nourishment personally in the dry, barren fields of famine.

Just under ten years ago my friend Sandy and I decided to study together. We did the math and figured that if we studied two chapters a week we could finish the whole Bible in eleven years. We are nearly through as I write this chapter. At the time, I remember thinking how cool it was to have found a person who would actually commit to studying the Bible all the way through. But I had no idea how life-sustaining the truth there would be.

After all, I knew the Bible. I had even minored in Bible through college. But I had no idea as to the power it would have in my life. With His words, the truth, God walked me through each week of what would turn out to be the most challenging ten years of my life. He saw me through loss, famine, death, and life lived at such a demanding pace that it threatened to take me out. In all those places He has met me, and I have found truth. And most of all, I have found the food to live out those famines. Each week, no matter what we are studying, it is precisely what I need. He meets me there because He knows the exact words I need to hear; He sees me and knows what food will satisfy that famine in my heart. It is long past the time where I could even articulate a request. But He knows, and He gives nourishment to me personally, intimately, and powerfully.

I will never forget how He did this for me during one of the hardest weeks of my life, when I realized my marriage was coming to an end. My study that week fell in one of the least read parts of the Bible. If I had wanted to look for a promise for what my family was going through, I never would have looked there.

But there it was, right smack dab in the middle of my chapter. A king in Israel was preparing his people for a battle. He brought them all together and prayed, "God, we don't know what to do, but our eyes are on you."[5] Now that is an amazing promise—that even when we do not have the answers, we can find them when we look to God.

I went to my guys several months after that devastating week as we were still reeling from the fall-out. I told them, "Guys, I did not expect this to happen. This one shocked me, but it did not shock God. Look at where He has me studying. Look at the promise He gave me."

My boys and I have held to that promise for years now. And through those years I often have truly not known what to do, but I have stood in the field and somehow kept my eyes on Him.

Not long ago in my study I came across another guy who had a unique and intimate understanding of famines. His name was Elijah. Elijah was the prophet who told the wicked King Ahab of Israel that there would be no rain until he gave the word.[6] After he told the king of the coming lack of rain, thus creating his own famine by his very obedience, Elijah went to the place where God provided for him. Ravens brought him meat, and there was a brook for water. But day after day, as the famine persisted, the brook began to dry up.

Have you ever experienced that? Have you stepped out in obedience only to find a famine as the outcome of your obedience? And as one day turned to another, you watched that brook dry up, your resources dwindling, knowing all the while you had done what God asked. You had been obedient, but it still was not enough, because you were hit like everyone else by the famine. You don't want to escape the famine, you don't want to close your heart to it, you are willing to feel it. But the reality exists. There is no food, there is no rain, and the brook is drying up.

There are many circumstances in our life that can put us in this situation. I am learning that in these places it is less about the needs of the moment and more about obedience. At such times, we may resolve to go it on our own, or we can surrender and tell ourselves and others God is really enough and obeying Him is what we do. We may say following Him gives unwavering direction for our lives and that serving Him is what we get out of bed for.

Well, guess what? That should be, must be true of each of us. When we say that, we are making it clear that, like Elijah, we will tell the king all we are supposed to tell him and sit by that brook until it dries up. Most often we will be sitting there alone—alone in a famine of our own creation and alone in our obedience. It is in those quiet moments, as we watch the ground dry up and form cracks where water once flowed, that we truly know how much we are depending on God. And in those moments when there is not enough, we can truly experience that He is sufficient. In fact, He is not just enough, but somehow more than enough.

Of course, you can also feel something very different as you sit by that dried up brook. You can feel a deep and sickening sense of panic. Fear can overwhelm you, because to the depths of your gut you know you are alone in your obedience. Your thoughts tell you that your actions in following God have taken you far beyond where others want to go. You are totally alone to the core of your spirit and you feel it.

You said the correct words. You made the right choices. You did all the right things. But as you sit by the brook, watching it dry up, you realize you did all that—but now you are very alone and desperate for water. You have done the hard part, you have been obedient. You are not digging through the mud for water, nor are you going to a foreign place to find it. You have not closed your heart off; you have let nothing die. You are right where He asked you to be. Now "Be still,"⁷ or in other words, cease striving, and know He is God.

Just be still. I know you are tired. In fact, you may be so tired that, just to find some water, you are starting to look at what Moab might hold for you. Just stop, rest, exhale, and listen to Him. Listen to what He is saying about you, to you. Listen to what He is asking you to do next.

I spend many days in the field like Elimelech. I also spend more days than I can count like Elijah, sitting by a stream that is all but dried up. I can tell you almost verbatim what my prayers sound like at those moments. The words are less important than the heart that is pouring them out. And at the core, what my heart feels is complete loneliness. I am alone with my thoughts and fears, alone with my burdens, and most of all, alone with my pain. I know that most often those thoughts come as I sit and endure a famine my own obedience has created. I am a single mom with a lot of big boys, boys I love with all that is in me. And at times they require all that is in me. They are boys I desire to raise up to not only honor God, but to reflect Him to a world in need. Because of his disabilities, my son Cameron has required not only attention, but tremendous physical strength, patience, and almost constant care. And in the midst of all that, I have been alone. I am choosing, out of obedience to the unique set of circumstances in my life, to remain alone.

On most days that is okay. On most days there is so much going on that I hardly notice there is no one there beside me. But there are days and there are moments when it all comes at me like a flood, except that there is no water. There is only the dry ground that cracks beneath my feet, and the constant churning in my gut that tells me my stream is drying up. It's at those moments I look over at the hills of Moab. I watch a ridiculously romantic movie or I see another one of those unreal commercials that almost make you cry because they are so melodramatic. Or it could be as simple as an old man taking the hand of his elderly wife and helping her out of the car. My heart aches for that and my mind wanders to what that would be, could be, and should be like. I think about what it would feel like to be held, to have someone care about me, and to have someone else take the violent blows my son dishes out—just for a night. I think about what it would be like to have someone who is strong and steady or to have someone who is just like the guy in the movies. I feel that ache because I am in a famine, and there is something I was created to need that I do not and likely will not ever know again: the security, protection, or companionship of a husband.

A while back I was having one of those times when such thoughts were going through my mind. At the same time, in the span of three days God brought me five different women who sat with me face to face and told me almost the same story. Their husbands were leaving, and they were alone and afraid.

Do you know what I told each of those women as I looked them deeply in the eyes? I told them God was enough and that He was able to meet them in that dry and dusty field. He was enough to give them all they needed, all they desired, and all they hoped for. He would meet them where they were, and in that desperate place He would be enough.

It was true. I knew it, but it was not until I got alone with God for a quiet moment after I left the last of the five women that He spoke so clearly to my heart, "*Becky, if you will stay in this famine I will not only meet you there, but I will use you from there.*" The truth of that hit the depths of my heart. I could look those women in the eyes and tell them that God was enough because, despite my times of lonely famine, He really is there for me. He really is all I have. There is nothing else and no one else. Through the good days, bad days, days that are full, and days that are lonely, He is all I depend on. Or I could look at those women and tell them to just wait, and in a couple of years maybe God would bring someone else into their lives and then they would be okay. But that is not what you learn in the famine. You learn that *He* is enough. You must stay in that place of longing, not going to Moab, and not letting that longing die. It is in that place, when the ground cracks beneath your feet and the brook dries up, that you can know your Creator in ways you never imagined. It is when you are still that you really know what it means that He is God.

There is nothing wrong with finding a good man; it can be a great blessing. But you will never find him in Moab. You will never find him if you are running away from your famine. If that is God's plan, He will bring that man to you in the field or beside the brook. Or maybe, just maybe, He will not bring a man; maybe He will come alone. And may I tell you, there is nothing like it when He comes to those broken, exhausting, lonely moments and gives us what we never imagined asking for – Himself.

There is nothing like it when He walks right up to us, just like Peter and John did to the crippled man, and looks into our eyes. He sees the pain, and better, knows what caused it. And even before we can get the words out of our mouths to tell Him how much change we need, He is showing us how to walk. He is strengthening our faith. He is meeting our need. He is filling the gap. He is erasing the deficit.

Does that make the famine go away? Sometimes it does. But at times He just comes to us in the middle of the famine to remind us that He is still here and will meet our needs. He will always provide food. Week after week I have seen the truth of that in His Word as He has walked me through the last ten years, taking me through hundreds of chapters and thousands of verses, with each promise coming at the right time, each for the right reason.

PEOPLE

God is enough for us in the famines of our lives. He brings what we need, but not necessarily what we want. We are pretty sure the two are the same, that what we want is actually what we need. But we really are not the best judge of that; He is.

I love what my friend Pat says, "We don't even know what we don't know." Since it seems abundantly clear that "knowing" is not our strength, we better start believing that He does know and that He does not necessarily provide what we find best or what we want, but what we actually need.

God's provision is right on time and right on target. He can provide for us alone, as He did for Elijah at the brook, or He can use people, as He showed Elijah next. God came to him as the brook dried up and gave him what he needed to survive the next season of famine. He told him to go to see a certain widow who was caring for her son[8] and that she would provide for him throughout the rest of the famine.

This seemed to be a strange command. A widow, after all, would barely have the resources to nourish herself, let alone a stranger. Still, Elijah, a man who had just been fed by ravens, was more than willing to believe that God could use her. But as Elijah walked into her village and called to her from the town gate, the widow herself was less than willing to believe that this man could help her. I would not blame her, as he was kind of demanding in their first encounter. He calls to her to bring him some water and then tells her, "While you are at it, give me a piece of bread." Her response is telling for a woman who has lived through many famines and is about to give up on this one. She tells him she has only a little water and enough supplies to make a single loaf of bread for herself and her son, and then they are going to die.

How is that for hospitality? She was done, through, finished. At this point, the man calling out to her was another frustration she could not even acknowledge. Elijah's response is interesting. The first thing he tells her is not to be afraid. He tells her that if she would just do what he asked, she would have enough food not only for one day but for the entire famine. He did not ask her to believe it, he did not ask her if she wanted to, he just asked her to do it.

Well, she obeyed. Can you imagine how hard it would be for her to walk into that house, to see her son, and then to begin preparing this meal for someone else while her own stomach groaned? She walked the food out to Elijah anyway. I am guessing she was not smiling when she served him. But as she moved back into her house, her eyes fell on a full jar of flour and oil. As it turned out, she would make bread every day until the rain came, and always have enough. Elijah's faith strengthened her faith and enabled her to survive. God could have sent him anywhere, but He wanted to give to the widow. He saw her famine and sent someone to help her through it.

Don't you love it when God does that? When He comes to us through someone we love and encourages us to the core? What a gift that is. The people God gives us to love are a great source of encouragement in the famine. But God does not always use people to help us along. At times, when we have so little ourselves, He himself comes— and asks us to give something away. And we look at Him and say, "Are you crazy? Do you know I am about to die here, and you want me to use the little energy I have, the little money I have, the little time I have, to give to someone else?"

Yes, that is exactly what He wants you to do. One of the greatest methods God uses to help us through the famine is service. Giving to others takes the focus off ourselves. It does not make sense, we can't understand why, but somehow when we serve God because we love Him, because we want others to know Him, we hardly notice that all of a sudden we don't have that same growling in our stomachs. Suddenly those places running out of supplies seem to never be empty. In our poverty, in our weakness, God can use us. When we serve others in the middle of our own famines, we no longer feel sorry for ourselves.

I don't know about you, but I have made the widow's pathetic little speech before. It would sound a bit different, something like, "You want me to do that for you? Do you have any idea what is required to live my life everyday? I don't have time to take a breath, let alone do another thing." Our famines may not threaten our lives like her famine did. But they can still be as consuming. God used Elijah to pull her out of her pity party to see there were others doing without as well. And when her focus left herself and her son, so did the famine.

Can you see how God has done that for you? Can you think of a time when you were at the end of your rope, picking up the last pieces of wood to build a fire to cook your last meal? When you were ready to quit, until all of a sudden you saw someone else struggling just like you, and somehow you found the compassion to do something about it? You may not want to; you may not know why it's asked of you. But when you do it, amazingly you are filled to overflowing with love, joy, and most of all hope that maybe, just maybe, you will have enough to make it through the famine. And in the process you may be shocked to find that you actually have some joy. Not just a little, but enough to overflow to others as you give to them.

Living in famine is not about walking around in mourning. It simply means you live the life that is put in front of you. We all live the outcome of our own choices, the choices of others, and God's choices. The reality of that can be daunting, but it can also be exciting. I can promise you it will not be boring. When you live in the famine, not escaping it and not protecting yourself from it, you live life at its fullest, deepest, and highest.

FAMINE IN A GARDEN

No one knew that kind of life better than Jesus. Jesus lived life in loss and grief, and He lived in abundance and joy. He knew all about famine. He lived for 40 days without food, not escaping when He was tempted, not protecting Himself. He felt it all—the pain of loss, the discouragement, and the disappointment in others. He was loved and He was hated. And in the end, the very people He came to save rejected Him.

He lived his life in famine. People did not come even close to meeting His needs. He never expected them to. Talk about a gap, a deficit! Jesus had a huge hole that only God could fill, and He knew how to let God do that – until the day in the Garden of Gethsemane[9] just outside the city of Jerusalem. It was there in the garden that He faced a famine He had never known – separation from His father. He was about to take the sin of the world on His shoulders, to carry it, and to pay for it. He would feel it all and endure it all. As He cried out to God His Father, pouring His heart out, sweating drops of blood, He asked for another way. He asked if this cup could pass from Him. Did He really have to endure this famine?

Yes, He did. He had to. He could not go to Moab. He could not protect himself. He had to do it and He had to feel it all. There was no other way to bridge the gaping hole, to fill the deficit, and to meet the need of all mankind. Because, you see, there is a universal famine each one of us is born into. It is our sinful nature. We all are born with a huge need, a hole. In fact, we are born with a chasm impossible for us to cross. But He was willing. That moment in the garden He made a choice to end that famine for all time. His sacrifice on the cross would close the gap, fill the need, and end that particular famine, the greatest famine we would ever know. He ended that famine on the cross for all people, for all time.

RECAPTURE

I was in the middle of one of my deepest, darkest famines several summers ago. Challenge faced my boys and me on every front. We were a mess. Nothing was working out right. Cameron's struggles had reached a new level of intensity. Our budget was upside down. Schoolwork and housework were piling up faster than my laundry. Life felt totally out of control.

In the middle of that summer, I came across these amazing words in my study, words that stopped me in my tracks. I was in the middle of another obscure book of the Bible that you can barely find, let alone quote from. And in the middle of that book I read these words from God: "I will do *this* to recapture the hearts of the people."[10] (italics mine) I could fill in the "this" for God, no problem. I will use Cameron to recapture your heart, Becky. I will use your checkbook that will not balance to recapture your heart. I will use your house that has no order, your chores that are not done, your life that feels out of control—yes, Becky, I will for sure use all of that to recapture your heart.

Whatever or however that simple word "this" is defined in our lives, it will almost certainly contain famine of some kind. And it is the very thing God uses to recapture our hearts. Our hearts are wild, passionate organs that we struggle to control. They are that part of us that often wants the wrong things from the wrong places. It is our hearts that most want to escape the famine. In fact, our hearts perpetually have their bags packed for Moab. They are where we feel most deeply and where God can use us the most. He wants our hearts and He will do everything to get them. He will give and He will take. He will be God, and He has earned the right to your heart and mine. He made an impossible choice. He ended our greatest famine, the one that separated us from Him. He sent His one and only Son to die for us because He loved us so much. Now as we endure our famines, we can know He is using each one of them to bring us closer to Him, to recapture our hearts.

That is exactly His intention for Naomi as we watch her sit alone in Moab, enduring indescribable loss and a new kind of famine.

Chapter Two

Death

Now Elimelech, Naomi's husband, died, and she was left with her two sons. They married Moabite women, one named Orpah and the other Ruth. After they had lived there about ten years, both Mahlon and Kilion also died, and Naomi was left without her two sons and her husband.[1]

I CAN REMEMBER the day like it was yesterday. I sat in a large preschool room with my son Cameron. The room was brightly decorated with large windows on one side. At quick glance you would have taken it for almost any preschool classroom. But if you looked closely, you would see subtle signs that this room was very different, created with care for children with distinctively different needs. As I sat there with my son, taking in the room while waiting for the Program Specialist, I began to notice some of the differences, and a state of unsettledness began to sweep over me. When Karen walked in, she smiled and first introduced herself to three-year-old Cameron, looking at him for a long time. I followed her eyes as they took in my little boy, his brown curly hair, his dark blue eyes, his face full of freckles. He was wearing his best outfit for his morning of testing at the preschool for special needs children.

I had come there almost as a formality. I wanted to rule out any severe disability and attribute Cam's lack of response to his being one of a set of busy triplets. But even as Cam went through his thirty minutes of testing in the afternoon, I could see he was not doing what the instructor asked. He frequently had that far-away look that characterized him so often when he played at home. As Karen began to speak to me she did not even mention the words "rule out." In fact, the testing had given clear confirmation that Cameron was severely autistic as well as retarded. She continued to talk and show me charts and graphs, tables and statistics. She was so kind, but I heard very few words after her first sentence. I sat there with my arm protectively around my son, not even beginning to comprehend what life was going to look like. I asked several lame questions out of total ignorance, like "When will he start acting normal? Will he ever catch up? Will he be okay after two years here, and can he then start kindergarten with his two brothers?" She was so kind, responding with absolute patience and the tenderness that demonstrated complete understanding of what I was trying to wrap my heart around. The questions that were screaming in my mind and heart were more like "Will he ever talk? Will he ever be potty-trained? Will he ever be safe around others or even himself? And most of all, will I ever understand what in the world God was thinking when He allowed Cam to live with this disability?"

All I knew is that every dream I had for my son had just died. I did not know at that moment as I sat with Cam, listening to Karen, how many things I would be left with and, at the same time, left without. I had no idea as a young mom what the future would hold. I did not grasp at that moment that in the future he would not be small and three years old. He would be thirteen, twenty three, fifty three, and seventy three. And at each of those ages he would be without most of what he would need to function safely in life. I had no idea as I held his little hands that some day those fingers would scratch and claw at me in fear and frustration. I had no idea that those deep blue eyes would always stay so vacant and in their loss of understanding would bring pain beyond comprehension to those who most loved him. I never imagined the strength and drive he would have with his two-year-old mind in the body of a young teenager. And I could never have dreamed that I would be handling him alone.

I did not realize it that day, but I had just begun the deepest, most painful, permanent famine I would ever know. Nor did I realize that what God had done for me that day as I sat in the middle of that preschool classroom was unveil the most powerful tool He would use to recapture my heart – my son, Cameron.

DEATH LEAVES YOU WITH AND WITHOUT

Death must have thousands of words dedicated to describing the loss that it holds for the heart of a person. But I love the simplicity of the two phrases used in the short account of Naomi's loss. Death left her with and death left her without. Is that ever the truth! Death leaves you with more to do. Death leaves you without the strength to do it. That is as simple and sad as it gets.

For Naomi, death left her with two sons, and death left her without a husband to share them with. Death left her with two weddings he did not see, with two young men he could not help raise. Death left her family without financial stability and without its head. She was left without the man who chose to leave the famine to go to Moab, so death even left her without a villain. She was left without a man who could say, "I am sorry I put you in this place, Naomi. I am sorry for having come to Moab in the first place. Not only did my choice cost you our future together, but eventually even our sons." Death left her with incredible hurt, pain, and loss, and death left her without someone to blame.

What has death left you with? You may have experienced the physical death of someone who shared your life. But that is not the only kind of death we experience. There are many other kinds as well. Like the death of a relationship, your health, your finances, or job security. It might be the death of dreams or the death of your childhood. What have those deaths left you with? Are you left with more work, more heartache, more questions to answer, or more bills to pay? Or possibly those deaths have left you with more fear, worry, doubt, more gray hair, a few more pounds, or more wrinkles. Sometimes it is simply that death leaves you without the ability to cope with life.

It is true that death takes and takes. But it also gives and gives. And at the moment death occurs, you have no idea of all it has left you with; nor can you begin to comprehend what it has left you without. Those two parallel truths will be lived out as you grieve your loss in some form for the rest of your life. One thing is absolutely certain: no matter what kind of death you experience, you are always left with grief.

Grief is an agonizing thing. As we experience the death of something or someone we love, we instantly know and experience grief for that loss. And as much as we can become immediately aware of the pain associated with grief, the reality of that grief will continue to unfold itself as we live our lives without something significant, powerful, and important to us. As we grieve a death, there are moments that hit us to the very core of who we are.

At times that wrenching pain is reflected in loud and deep tears; other times there is only the silent cry of our hearts, when tears don't seem to be enough to express how our hearts are breaking. At those moments I believe God does one of two things in our hearts: He either grows in immense proportions to be able to contain such pain or He becomes obsolete to us. He is either a God who will be so huge that He can still be worshipped in our pain or He is another in the long line of things that have disappointed us when we most needed Him. Death is powerful. Death leaves you with searing pain, but it does not leave you without an all-loving, tender-hearted God – a God so huge He will go with you to the depths of your pain, understand it, and lovingly walk you through it. But as you begin to look at some of the possible kinds of death you have experienced, there is one question that must be asked. Do you want Him there? Or would you rather grieve without Him?

DEATH OF A PERSON

Although death leaves us with many things, what breaks our hearts most is what death leaves us without. The death of a spouse leaves you without a future together. All the plans, hopes, and dreams you made are now gone. You are left with only the memory of that person. But most of all, death leaves you without the person close to you. He or she is no longer physically there. You can't sit down to have a cup of coffee together. You can't laugh together at a funny movie. You can't find safety and warmth in his or her arms during the dark, cold nights.

I have friends who are widows. Some were young women when their husbands died; others were older. Regardless of their ages or how long they were married, their response is almost always the same. Death has left them without the man they loved and planned to spend the rest of their lives with. Death has left them alone, alone with their memories, alone with their daily struggles, and alone with their future plans. And they feel it, from dealing with broken sprinklers, to planning for college, to handling grandchildren. They are left without the one person who wanted to share it all—and with whom they wanted to share it.

But there is Someone who still wants to share it all. In fact, He will even use *this* loss to recapture your heart. Because God alone knows how you feel. He chose to endure the death of His own Son. He chose to feel it. In fact, He felt it so deeply and acutely that He actually took that deep pain out of it for us. God took the separation out of death. That is the part that hurts so much; you are separated from the person you love. But you are not left without hope, and that separation need not be permanent, because Jesus made a way for you to see the person you love again. Let me tell you about an extraordinary man for whom heaven and this truth were so strikingly real. His name is Dr. Clyde Cook.

Dr. Cook was the president of Biola University for many years, including the four years I attended there. He was a wonderfully personable man who took the time to stop and talk to students, share a meal with them, and hear their struggles and concerns, their hopes and fears. It seemed he knew every student by name. I noticed that when I was a student as well as during the times I had the chance to visit with him later. Dr. Cook and his wife, Anna Belle, remained a part of my life over all the years since I graduated from Biola. My boys also had the chance to spend time with him, something I am so grateful for.

Dr. Cook passed away in the spring of 2008, less than a year after he retired as president of Biola. It was news that was grieved by thousands of former students as well as by friends and family. His memorial service provided a way for many to celebrate his life and reflect on the memories they had of this vibrant man, and also to grieve his loss.

Several years before his death Dr. Cook had arranged to make an audio tape that would be played at his memorial service. So in the middle of the various speeches that day in an overcrowded church with thousands more watching online, Dr. Cook's picture appeared on the screen and his distinctively calm voice spoke his very special message. It was surreal, to say the least, to hear his voice at his own funeral. After greeting us in his typically humorous way, he began to describe what he was experiencing in heaven. Reading from the last book of the Bible, the book of Revelation, he painted a vivid picture of what he was seeing, as we sat in chairs, trying to imagine such wonder. After his description, he shared several things with his family and friends regarding his love and desires for them. And at the very end Dr. Cook did an amazing thing.

The last thing he said was addressed to a specific group of people. He knew that there would be some at his service who did not have any relationship at all with God. As he closed he wanted to share with them one last time that he had a great desire to see them again. And he knew that maybe as they sat at the service they would stop and consider their own lives. In those very personal, very quiet moments, he reminded them in his gentle way that the death of Jesus had literally ended their famine, taken the deep pain out of death, had made a way not only to see those we loved again, but to spend eternity with God Himself. He wanted them to hear it from him one more time, because even though they were grieving him now, the separation did not have to be permanent.

There were many great speakers that day and there was tremendous music, but it was those short five minutes when Dr. Cook's own voice filled the room that created the most comfort for my heart. I was reminded that the death of this great man had left us all with grief, but not without hope.

DEATH OF A RELATIONSHIP

There are other deaths in our lives not so clearly understood. There is no graveside to walk away from, no closure. There is pain and there is loss, but there are few answers. Certainly divorce holds that kind of death.

Divorce or the death of any relationship leaves us without the past we loved and without the future we hoped for. It reaches in and pulls out the memories we cherish and contorts them, making them no longer enjoyable. Divorce leaves you without the family photos you displayed. It leaves you without confidence, without self-esteem, without money, and without someone to sleep beside you at night. And it leaves you with children who are torn apart. It leaves you with awkward sporting events, weddings, graduations, funerals, and birthdays. Divorce can leave you with bitterness and anger, with depression and disillusionment. It can leave you with angry, confused teenagers and without someone to help you raise them. It can send you into famine. It can rob you for the rest of your life.

Or you can look at it differently. You can choose to see that the death of a marriage leaves you with God as your spouse. It leaves you with an opportunity to learn forgiveness in a way you never thought you could. It leaves you without anyone to depend on except God. Divorce leaves you with famine, that is true, but it also leaves you with countless opportunities to minister to others struggling in the same place. Divorce leaves you with choices, many choices. You must choose to allow God to hold your heart, because without question, divorce will leave you with a broken one. But it does not have to leave you without hope, joy, or expectancy. He will use even *this* to recapture your heart in a way you never would have dreamed.

But in order for Him to recapture it, your heart must first be soft enough for Him to firmly but lovingly hold it. I have talked with many women in the midst of this life-changing experience, and one of the first things I tell them is that they need to find a place and time when their kids are safely cared for. Then they need to go into the house or car or wherever and fall apart for a while. They need to feel it! Death of a relationship may leave you with anger and bitterness, but that is not all it has left you with. Beneath that fire is pain, scorching pain. Unless you are willing to feel that pain, you will stay conveniently in your anger. After all, who wants to feel pain when you can be just plain mad!

I sure did not. Give me anger a million times over pain! But as much as I seemed to find some kind of weird soothing comfort in being mad, my heart felt strangely hollow as I nursed my anger and the growing resentment I felt. It was not until I had my very first weekend at home alone after my divorce that I let God open a brand new door. As much as I was horrified to see what was behind that door, it was a life-changing process to feel the pain beneath my anger.

In the weeks after my divorce I had stayed very busy caring for my guys and putting out fires everywhere. It was not until that Friday of the first weekend, when they were all gone at the same time, that it hit me. I was in the parking lot at Trev's high school. It was the middle of July, and I had just watched his summer league basketball game. As I slowly walked to my car alone, I knew what was facing me after my short two-mile drive home. An empty house. A huge, cavernous two-story house with five bedrooms full of memories I did not want to face. A house filled to the brim with pain I did not want to feel.

I reached my car and as I opened the door I felt a new hope for a last reprieve. I would call my friend Sandy and ask her if I could come over and spend some time there instead of going home. My very kind and caring friend told me no! I was shocked. I tried to explain to her that I was very discouraged and simply did not want to face that empty house. She wisely, lovingly, and firmly told me I needed to face those walls, that vacant house, those thoughts and painful memories.

With my last recourse gone, I drove slowly out of the parking lot in the direction of my house. I pulled into the garage and opened the door I had walked through every single day for many years. The door I carried newborn triplets through. The door that opened with the excited voices of my sons as they came in from playing with their friends, their hearts full of new adventures to tell me about. But there were no voices as I opened the door that day. Only ominous silence.

I walked from room to room, thinking of all that had taken place inside those walls for a significant chunk of my life. As I moved through the house, I could feel a flood of emotion coming to the surface. I fought it back with all the strength I could muster, but it all came out as I opened the door to the master bedroom and fell on the floor and cried for more than two hours straight. It was that ugly kind of crying you never do in front of people. The kind of crying that leaves your eyes puffy and your head pounding.

I said few words in that time. I could not tell you what I was even thinking, but I can tell you I was feeling it all, every part of it. I was grieving the loss of my eighteen-year marriage; I grieved the dreams I hoped the future held, dreams that I now knew I would never see fulfilled. I felt the pain of the past and looked with dread at a future filled with new pain I otherwise never would have been able to imagine.

I had cried before that night, but those tears had been with and for my boys. It was not until Friday night that I allowed myself to feel the pain for me. For what I had lost. It was a long night. But after falling asleep from exhaustion, I woke with a heart that felt more whole and complete than it had ever been. In the years since that night, I have had my share of tears and frustrations over the death of my marriage, but I can assure you that none have lasted long. God has used even *this* to powerfully recapture my heart. But first my heart had to find the courage to open the door that held back the pain hidden beneath my anger. It was not pleasant, but the outcome was amazingly complete healing. And surprisingly, a new calmness, peace, and even a hint of hope for what God would do in the future.

DEATH OF DREAMS

The dreams we cultivate in our minds and hearts can be as different and individual as we are. They can include getting married, getting a promotion, having a new car, or having a great retirement. Depending on what the dream is, its death can be devastating. Because when dreams die, we lose not only the dream, but what we have defined that dream to mean in our lives.

One of those devastating losses must certainly be when the dream of having a child of your own dies. I have walked with several women through this process, and it is a deep and painful famine. I have marveled at the ways they have allowed God to meet them in this place where their greatest dream has died. The death of this particular dream leaves you without a person who would be a part of both you and your husband. It leaves you without company as you grow older, without weddings, without graduations, without grandchildren.

It can also leave you *with* other things, things you would not desire to have in your heart. It can leave you with resentment, bitterness, hardness, and anger. Most of those strong and powerful emotions are often directed at God Himself. They are normal, the right emotions for the death of this dream. And the right thing to do as God comes to you in this deeply felt famine is to give your feelings to Him—as loud and as long as you feel them. He can take it, He knows it, and He is hurting with you. Do that in whatever form is necessary. Write it down or cry it out from your knees, on your face, or wherever you find yourself in this pain. Let Him have it all. He wants it, He can contain it, and He *can*, even in this loss, recapture your heart.

I know that you probably are saying right now, "I don't want Him to recapture my heart; I just want a baby. Is that too much to ask? After all, I would love and take care of that baby. Why do so many women get pregnant who never want their children? In fact, having a baby is a nightmare to them. Yet here is my deepest and fondest dream, and He won't give it to me." But what is He giving you?

As He comes to us in the famine, we often do not get back what we lost or even what we ask for; He always gives us something better. We get Him. And we get Him in ways we could never imagine. He meets needs we didn't even know we had, and as He does, an amazing flood of peace comes over us. We don't get our way, which you would think would make us angry. But somehow it does not. In those precious moments when He meets us in the famine of our dying dreams, it is enough.

There is something so powerful that happens in our hearts when God does not give us what we want. Despite everything, we still want Him. Do you know what I mean? Our deepest, most profound desire is not met, and yet we are willing and somehow able to turn from the dream that has just shattered before our eyes and look into His face. We can't go to Moab, living our lives in bitterness and anger, and we can't close ourselves off and say we never wanted it anyway. We must take His hand and trust Him.

I love hearing that with enough faith we can see mountains move.[2] However, I am learning that sometimes the greater gift is when the mountain does not move, no matter how strong our faith. When our dreams die we are left with a huge, rocky mountain in front of us, but we are not left without a Guide. God comes to us at the foot of that mountain, that broken, dead dream, and puts out His hand. He tells us, "This one will not move, but I will guide you over it." That is the greater gift. That is truly better than having your dream met just the way you want it. To have Him personally and intimately walk you through the pain of loss will be something that will change who you are. And most of all, it will change what you dream. It hurts, I know that. But it's a healing kind of pain, and you can do it.

So pour it all out to Him. Ask Him to move the mountain, to give you the dream, and just lay your heart wide open for Him to see it all. But if the mountain stays, be willing to take the first step with Him and see what He has left you with—a recaptured heart.

DEATH OF HEALTH

For some, the death they endure is very personal; it is the death of their own health. The death of health leaves you with exhaustion, pain, and almost constant discouragement. When your health dies, it also leaves you without answers, without hope, without the drive, will, and determination that used to fuel you. It is so difficult to watch someone who had incredible vitality and even amazing passion for service lose that spirit as their health is failing. It is especially hard to see that in a young person. But regardless of your age or diagnosis, God can truly use this, too, to recapture your heart if you are willing. He will give to you in that place of famine in ways you cannot imagine, and He will use you powerfully to minister to others.

If you go to church any Sunday morning at Grace Community in Riverside, California, you will be greeted by a handsome couple sitting behind an information desk. The man's name is Bo. He is a distinguished, white-haired gentleman with a magnetic, infectious smile. His wife is named Pat. She is kind, friendly, and energetic. They resemble so many likeable people you might meet at any church. But when you walk up closer to ask them a question, you will quickly see that there is more to this couple than the obvious joy they demonstrate.

Bo sits in a specially made electric wheelchair that he controls with his chin. He is almost completely paralyzed. He was in an accident over 50 years ago when he was an athletic college student exercising on a trampoline. He passed out from the accident, then woke up and walked home. He graduated, went to Korea to serve his country, returned to go to school to be a physical therapist, and began a practice. He married Pat and they had three children. He did not give the accident a second thought as he lived a normal, healthy life.

But one morning seven years after the accident, when Pat said goodbye to Bo as he left for work, she noticed as he walked to his car that he was dragging his foot. She asked him about it and of course he said it was nothing. But Pat had been an occupational therapist before leaving her career to raise their three small children. She immediately called some doctors, and Bo went to see them later that day. Tests were done, and they found that a bone had been dislodged during his trampoline accident years before and was pressing against his spine. He had surgery in 1965 and later had two more operations to try to repair the damage. The doctors met with the couple after the final surgery and told them they had done all they could to fuse the bone, but said that the injury would cause progressive degeneration of his spine.

They soon began to realize what the surgeons meant, as Bo began to slowly lose strength in his legs. He continued his physical therapy practice, but they could see that it was going to be possible for only a short time. So they made the decision in the fall of 1968 that Pat would go to school at night and on weekends to get her teaching credential.

In the next few years, Bo retired as a physical therapist. He said with his typical self-effacing humor that he had to leave his practice, or his patients would be helping him off the ground. I met them a few years later as we went to the same church for a short time. I remember them so well. He was walking with a cane at the time, and each Sunday their family came into church together. They were such a handsome couple and always had so much dignity. I know them even better these thirty years later because my little sister married their oldest son fifteen years ago. As the years passed, I watched the strength slowly leave the lower portions of Bo's body to the point where he now requires total care and has very limited use of his hands.

Bo has endured a death in his health, a famine that will last for the rest of his life, but I can assure you that God has met Bo and Pat in the famine.

Pat told me recently that when they first got married they were "Sunday Christians," going to church just because they were supposed to. She said Bo's condition caused them to be not only daily Christians, but "minute-ly" Christians. They are totally dependent on God for everything. I have marveled at the sacrificial care and love Pat has shown Bo all these years. He receives her help with equal love and gratitude. Their relationship is covered in dignity, both in giving and receiving. Pat will tell you that they have been given so much more than they lost. It does not even come close. Sure, Bo is not able to get down on the floor to play with his grandchildren, but what he demonstrates for them is so much greater. He exhibits the quiet dignity that clothes those who live in the famine, who endure the death of something they need, and yet are left with more.

I have learned so much from the way they have endured their famine. Pat says the key is "preparation equals peace." Preparation for them includes everything from determining where his meds are packed in case of an earthquake to having the forms ready to give the medical workers in the Emergency Room. However, their peace not only comes from those tangible preparations, but from the intangible ones as well.

They have in every way prepared their three children for whatever life holds as they all have learned to demonstrate sacrificial love. They have also prepared their hearts as they focus on what is to come for both of them: heaven. We need hope to endure the death of our health. Not only do *we* need that; even Jesus needed it in the most impossible famine of His life when He was dying on the cross. He could only make it through by thinking of what was to come for Him; he endured the cross because of the joy set before Him.[3] The hope of what is to come should generate in us the ability to not only endure, but to have a little bit of that joy, even in famine, even without health. One visit to the welcome desk at Grace Community will show you perfect evidence of that.

DEATH OF YOUR CHILDHOOD

Maybe for you the death you deal with is not created by something fresh or even something you can totally understand, but it has forever altered how you live your life. Like other deaths, the death of your childhood will leave you with and it will leave you without. If your childhood was taken away, you are powerless to alter what has happened. You are left without it, and most likely you are left with incorrect ways of dealing with life.

The death of your childhood could come in many forms. Someone you trusted may have defiled you, leaving you with shame and doubt and without one of the precious gifts God gave you to enjoy—the ability later in life to fully enjoy the intimacy He desired you to experience with your spouse.

Someone may have damaged you in other ways. Maybe you were abused physically or emotionally by your parent, and whether that abuse was with hands or words, the pain of it leaves you without self-worth and without confidence. And most of all, it leaves you without a will to say, "No, stop it. You cannot hurt me like that." You are left as an adult without a voice, and you continue to be a victim. You are left with a need to please that will overwhelm and consume your life. You will be left with guilt each time you enjoy yourself, because there must be something else you could, should, or would be doing *if* you were a good person. You are left with the blame for everything. And you will believe it, because you were never good enough as a child. So why not believe that as an adult you are capable only of messing things up? No matter what has caused the death of your childhood, no matter what kind of abuse you suffered, the overwhelming result is that you are left without rest, because you can never stop.

A while back there was a little phrase that jumped out at me when I was studying the time Israel left Egypt. While wandering in the desert, the Israelites were provided daily with food from God called manna— nourishment that literally fell from heaven. The passage describes God giving Moses directions for how they were to gather the manna. It is one of those sections in the Bible you tend to check out on when reading. It is a passage you think cannot apply to you, since you have never seen manna. Nor would you need to be told how much of it to gather, nor would you need to be given a cooking lesson on it.

But I remember that when I hit that section in my study, all of a sudden one little phrase jumped off the page at me. God had told Moses to have the people gather a certain amount of manna every day and had told him how they were to prepare it. Then God told him that on the sixth day the people were to gather double the amount of manna, cook it, and have it ready for the Sabbath, the day of rest.[4] That sounds like it makes sense, pretty logical stuff.

But then came the little phrase that knocked me out; it appeared at the tail end of this verse: "But some people went out and gathered on the seventh day and they found nothing."[5] Did you hear that? They gathered on the seventh day, and they found nothing. You know, those people had already physically picked up the manna the day before, not just for the sixth day but for the seventh day also. They had not only gathered it; they also had cooked it. It was sitting right there on the table as they walked past it to get their basket, opened the door, and headed outside for more gathering. And the truth is, they found nothing. Do you know why they found nothing? Because they were gathering when they should have been resting.

Have you ever done that? We all can do it; it can happen when we get too focused on work. But you know who does that all the time? In fact, who does it every chance they get? Those people who lost their childhoods. Such people are left without the ability to stop and without rest. Is that a description of you?

Think about it. When was the last time you woke up weary, because you are always exhausted, even when you sleep all night? You wake up and pull your clothes on for another day. You are really tired because yesterday you worked extra hard for some reason, but you don't remember why. As you shuffle through your kitchen you notice extra bread on the table. But it does not register because you walk right by that provision and get your bag to head out to do something, anything except rest. And what you find outside that door is nothing. You are gathering when you should be resting—and you find nothing.

We know a lot more than Moses did about the importance of that food. Manna was just a foreshadowing of the ultimate bread of life that would come – Jesus.[6] And we have to make a conscious choice to get up and walk in the light of what He has done for us. That bread is sitting right there on the table; yet we ignore it, brush past it, walk on by it, to find our baskets and go out the door.

Listen to me; will you please just stop? The next time you start past that table filled with bread will you just say "No, I don't need to do this today; I can rest"? That means you can stop staying up until three A.M. baking those cupcakes. It means you don't have to exercise four hours a day. You do not need to scoff at your reflection each time you catch it in a mirror or window. It means you could maybe, just maybe, sit on your couch, read a magazine, or watch a movie even if the floor is not vacuumed, the laundry is not folded, and the dishwasher is still full. And you can enjoy it. Maybe you can just rest. You are grown up now. You are the parent. So be a good one, especially to yourself. This is not easy. In fact, it might be the most difficult thing you will ever have to learn, but you can learn it. And without question, God will especially use *this* to recapture your heart.

I have heard it said that when you grow up in a loving, safe home you are given a mark that almost nothing in life can erase. You know who you are and you can face life confidently, no matter what comes at you. You will be prepared to make it through. But it is equally true that when you grow up in a home that is not safe, where there is abuse of any kind, or where parents are unkind, unjust, and inaccessible, you are given a different kind of mark, one that is equally powerful. And no matter what happens in the life of that child, good or bad, it filters through that marking, a marking that is nearly impossible for us to change on our own. But the good news is that God can give us another kind of mark. A mark that overrides the others. We can be marked, sealed with the Holy Spirit.[7] That mark is the most powerful of all.

Do you remember the word "recapture" in reference to the animal that has been marked and sent out into the wild, only to be captured again? That is exactly what God is saying when He tells us we have the mark of the Holy Spirit. We are in the wild, and life is truly that. We have one famine after another. But we are marked, and not just by the famines. Yes, we are left with markings and scars from the deaths we have endured, but we must be defined by *His* mark. We are not only defined by it; we are recaptured by it. He wants our hearts. As messy, dark, hard, and hurt as they are, He wants them. He will use even something you have lost, like your childhood, to recapture you. Will you let Him? Will you let Him help you grieve what you never even admitted had died in your life? Will you let Him hear your thoughts? Write them down or say them out loud so He can help you know which are true. Will you allow Him to help you forgive those who may never be sorry or even realize what they have killed in you? And most of all, will you let Him stop you at the door with your basket in hand, ready to gather another day? Will you let Him walk you over to the couch so you can rest with Him?

Once you decide to feel all that death has left you with, you can begin to learn how to truly worship God for what it has left you without.

DEATH, GRIEF, AND WORSHIP

In the years after Cam's diagnosis, each day held unique challenges. I want to take a few moments and have you step back with me as I unfold just one ordinary day in the life of this extraordinary boy. I really want you to feel with me the unique privileges as well as the challenges we faced. Please go back with me and experience such a day as though it were today.

After an often fitful night of sleep, I wake up and walk downstairs to a house that looks very different from the way I left it the evening before. Cameron has been awake and out of bed throughout the night. Each day I pour a series of pills into my son to control his behaviors. He takes eighteen pills every day. The total cost of medicating him is staggering, close to $150 a day, which, thankfully, is covered by insurance. Of those pills, four are designed just to help him sleep. And last night, on top of his normal medication, I gave him an additional two pills just to calm him down from the tantrum he was throwing at bedtime. Even with all those pills he was awake much of the night.

So as I walk downstairs through the salami strewn on the stairway and see the open two-liter bottle of soda on the table, I am reminded again of what died for me that day in the classroom—safety. I can look down at my forearms and see the result of his tantrum last night. I have over a dozen scratches from his outburst. Even after he bites and scratches me, he can look at the blood and have no idea how it got there.

In the last eleven years I have learned a new level of vigilance. Cameron has been everywhere in our neighborhood: pools, backyards, and boats, clothed and otherwise. He used to be very fast. Ten seconds looking away from him to get something for his brothers would allot him the chance to hop a fence and be in the pool of our neighbor. He does not fear what is dangerous for him, like a street, a cliff, or fire. Yet he is petrified of almost everything else. He does not understand cause and effect, which in the end hurts him the most as he tries to function in this world he does not understand.

Children like Cameron are almost never seen by the public. I do not take him out in public places; in fact, I stopped outings that would put him around crowds of people when he was about ten or eleven. He is a danger to himself and he is a danger to others. We are so accustomed to his outbursts that my boys and I just respond as if it were normal. It is only when someone comes to visit and sees him act out, sees him in a full tantrum, sees him break tables, chairs, sofas - it is only then, as we see the horror in their eyes, that we realize how very different our life is.

Now, on this typical morning, the house is finally picked up, my other boys are off on their various activities, and Cameron wakes up after finally having gone to sleep. He is content as he walks into the kitchen to find pancakes already made and waiting on a plate for him. He was dry through the night, and uses the bathroom correctly, which is always a celebrated victory. We play several spontaneous games together, he laughs and smiles a lot, and we settle in on the couch for our daily viewing of "Beauty and the Beast." As I sit there beside my son I am as thankful as I am exhausted by the opportunity I have been given to raise him. And I start another day in famine.

Cameron is now a young teenager, and he is a beautiful boy. He is not as tall and blonde as Logan; with his curly hair and fair complexion he looks more like Boone. He has the same cleft in his chin and the same captivating blue eyes as his brothers. He has a smile that warms your heart and dimples that come out when he really laughs. He has the strange and unusual beauty that inhabits those who keep their thoughts and feelings in secret. There is a sense of constant wonder about him as his life is covered in silence. He only uses one-word requests to communicate his desires. He never answers questions and never communicates his thoughts, feelings, or fears with words, only with actions.

When I look at him today I see the little boy who sat beside me in the classroom back then. He has the same curly brown hair, the same freckles, and sadly, the same level of confusion and distance in those blue eyes. We have lived a lifetime together in the last eleven years. And we have lived most of that time together in silence. I have cleaned up the contents of his diaper that he frequently smeared all over himself, his toys, the walls, the carpet. As I did, I silently cried out to God, "I hate doing this. I hate that he does it. I hate that he can't understand it. I hate the way it smells. I hate the way it looks. What were you thinking when you allowed this, God?" And as I silently fumed, my other little boys stood at the doorway with clean towels in hand, asking what they could do to help.

All I had to do was turn around and look at their sweet, loving, selfless faces to know the answer to my prayer. God could have said it out loud, but He did not have to. Their love for me and for their brother said it all. Yes, the death of Cam's future left us with a mess, struggles, and injuries. But it also left us with other things. It left us with love expressed in the most basic needs of life. Caring that went beyond what anyone could imagine has flowed through my other three boys to their brother. Death left them with character, love, and the ability to endure the events of each day with compassion.

I have sat with two six-year old-boys as they pored through the toy magazines before Christmas, looking for what they wanted to cut out and ask for from Santa. As they turned each page to find their favorites, they pointed to one toy after another and said, "This is not a good Cameron toy." They were not saying that he would not like to get it. They were saying they could not get it because Cam would break it or hurt himself with it. I watched as they turned each page, deciding on the best choice. But this was never done with disappointment. Instead, they showed a realistic hope that they would be able to enjoy something with their brother, not in spite of him.

There is no way to cultivate that kind of maturity in a child. It can only come in famine. It can only come when you are willing, even when you are small, to look death in the eye and have the courage to see what it has left you with and embrace it. There have been countless trips altered, vacations challenged, and outings ruined. Yet my boys have demonstrated a love for Cam that transcends their own obvious needs and desires. It is not his fault; he cannot control it. They see in him not only their brother, but a person who each day moves bravely through a world that overwhelms him.

Cameron's brothers defend him with all that is in them. Even if that means sending friends away who tease him. They have taken time and energy to try to help others know what life is like for Cam and for them. They have talked with social workers who interviewed us, newspaper reporters, and even people in the community. They are fair, they are clear, they are realistic, and they always show a maturity and level of mercy well beyond their years.

Once on a camping trip to Morro Bay, my nephew Jackson fell out of a tree and broke his arm in several places. We all went to the emergency room to wait with him. You can imagine that was not an easy place for eight-year-old Cam. Fortunately, we were the only ones in the waiting room, with the exception of an older couple sitting across from us. Cam bounced around a bit and made some squeals that were a bit loud, so I took him outside to walk around. I came back into the waiting room about five minutes later and saw my thirteen-year-old son Trevor sitting next to the older couple, talking with them. When we were finally called back, I asked him what he had been talking to them about. He told me the couple had said some things about Cameron, calling him a brat.

Trevor said, "I went over there to explain that Cameron has autism and he cannot control himself the way a normal boy could." I was amazed at his heart for his brother. I was amazed Trev protected Cam's dignity and his heart. Even though Cam would never know, Trev wanted them to understand. I can promise you that for as many times as I have cried out to God in anger and confusion, I have witnessed ten other times like this one where it is so clear. God was saying, "Becky, do you see? I am meeting you in this place. Your boys are not going without. In fact, they will be left with more than they would ever have known without Cameron in their lives."

I have seen growth not only in my boys; it also has been clear in the lives of the people we have been privileged to meet and work with because of Cameron. I have seen that God has much more planned than I could ever have imagined. There are teachers who, because of Cam, now have a relationship with God, and there's a bus driver as well. And in each case God is so clear as He says, "Isn't your struggle worth the cost, since those people now will spend eternity in heaven because they had the chance to know Cameron, to know his family, and most of all to know their Creator?" Yes, yes, a million times yes. I would not change what we have learned in this famine. I would not change the hearts of my other sons. I would not have missed knowing and encouraging those people or the countless others I get to speak to.

But the cry of my heart is for Cameron, "God, what about him, why does he have to suffer? Why does he have to live in a world he does not understand? Why does he have to hurt so much that he hurts others? Why?" I have poured out my heart to God as I lay on my face on the floor, exhausted and bloody from the simple act of trying to cut his nails. At the same time he is writhing on his bed, totally confused and afraid because he must feel with the pads of his fingers and not his nails. "God, it's so simple. It's the littlest of things, yet he cannot do it," I cry out. And it has been after those deep, dark moments, when I have cried until I have nothing left and have grieved a death that I watch every day, that I am silent and He speaks. Each time as I lie there alone, He comes to me in the famine. He comes to me in the part of my mother's heart crying out for my child and says "*I know. I know how this feels. I gave my Son, Becky. I gave my Son for you, for Cam, for Logan and Boone, and for Trevor. I gave Him up even after He pleaded with me for another way. I told Him no, death is the only way to leave them without condemnation and with hope. I did that for you and I called it love.*" Love is sure not what we would call it. Sometimes love does not feel good; it actually feels horrible. But it also feels right.

Love is almost never without pain. The truth to the core is that God is love, and we cannot define what love means without asking Him first. He has already shown us. "For God so loved the world that He gave...?"[8] What He gave was His one and only Son, and that caused His infinite heart pain we cannot begin to imagine. So in those moments of absolute desperation I have found peace. I don't really expect answers. I really don't know the questions I would ask anymore. I really just need peace at those times. I need to know that He is the strong arm that can hold me, and He not only understands but has a plan.

When God allows something like this in your life you can know it will be a clean cut, for God's choices always are. They hurt, but they heal. The choices of others tend to leave a jagged kind of scar that gets ripped open a lot. But God's cuts are pure, straight, and clear. And each of them comes with the assurance that in *this* He will recapture your heart.

Death always leaves us with and without. The second part of that statement has been the hardest part with Cam. I have learned that the toughest part of death of any kind is separation. We have looked at that in the other forms of death we have discussed. But I have learned it most deeply through the choices I have had to make for my son. Each choice creates separation and each separation creates a new way to grieve the death that brought this on.

Cameron's extreme and violent behaviors separated him from his brothers and me each weekend after he turned twelve, when a group home provided respite for us. This home gave us several nights in a row when we could go to bed knowing we would sleep the entire night. Several days of peace, calm, safety, and rest.

My boys and I did not want those days. In fact, we fought them until we had nothing left. But it was when we realized that we were drained and had no more resources left that we saw so clearly that this time not only helped us, but was necessary for our survival. So each Friday after school, the van took him to a group home instead of our house, and each Monday he was picked up from that home and taken to school. Each Friday afternoon at about 3:30 I looked at the clock and knew my son was reacting strongly to the fact that the van had just turned the wrong way and was no longer heading to our house.

In the summer I took Cam to the group home myself. And although I felt the moments each Friday during the school year when the van took him and I knew he was reacting, it was something altogether different to see it first-hand. Cam first tried to get me to turn around, which was often dangerous. When he knew it would not work, he simply started saying "home" and crying. You know, you could shoot me and it would not hurt as much. That was the worst. And I kept driving. And I walked him up to the door where the ladies greeted him with love and enthusiasm, then turned and walked back to my car grieving this loss, feeling the famine to the core.

As I drove away, I had some pretty intense talks with God. You know what He was telling me at those times when I had just separated my son from me and it was my choice? He told me it was the right thing, it was even love. And God was telling me He wants me to worship Him for that. Now that is a crazy thought, isn't it? God telling me to worship Him for one of the hardest things He ever asked me to do. But that is our God. And let me tell you, I am glad that He is so big that He can not only contain our pain but even in that pain deserves our worship.

Don't you want a God who is that big? A God who will not backpedal in the face of His choices as if to say; "Wow, I didn't know it would turn out that way. Sorry about that." No, our God is the kind of God who allows those hard places in our lives without apology. In fact, He lays those things in our lives and has the audacity to call it love. And He does it with the full intention of using them to recapture our hearts.

Is that the kind of God you know? Is that the kind of God you want to know? Or maybe right now you feel a little like closing this book and putting it on your shelf, because you don't really want to read any more about that kind of God. You don't want to hear about my son who is so handicapped or my friends who have suffered loss. You don't want to read about Naomi, or Ruth, or anyone else who had something hard in their lives in order for God to truly have their hearts. You are afraid. You don't want Him to allow something like that in your own life. Right now you are not totally sure that you even want your heart recaptured. In fact, you would like to run and hide. You would love to do anything to escape this famine!

I don't blame you a bit. There are days that, if I could, I would run and hide in the deepest, darkest cave I could find, just to pretend for a few minutes that I don't have to think, feel, or listen to what He is asking me to do. But you know that if I did that, He would find me. That is how much He loves me. That is how much He wants to recapture my heart. And somehow, even in the darkest and deepest days of my life, when He comes to me in that cave of my own creating and demands my worship for the very thing that sent me there, it feels right to give it to Him. In fact, it feels good. If you don't believe me, just ask Hannah.

HANNAH

Hannah was a woman who lived a few decades after Naomi and Ruth. She had a great home and a husband who was crazy about her. But she was in a famine. She had endured the death of a dream; she was living without. She had wanted a child for years, but after asking and asking she still was left with a broken heart and no child. She cried out to God, making a vow that if He would give her a child, that child would serve Him all the days of his life.[9] Serving Him would mean that her son would live in Shiloh and help the high priest, Eli. It meant her son would grow up somewhere else. Someone else would put him to bed at night. Someone else would love him, feed him, comfort him.

Perhaps in the depths of her mother's heart what was really crying out was, "Maybe someone won't comfort him. Maybe instead of love and care, he will be surrounded by insecurity, unkindness, and fear. Maybe instead of my loving hands, my son will feel pain at the hands of another." All those powerful emotions went into the vow she was making, but she was fully prepared to keep it.

Hannah was given a son; his name was Samuel. He would grow to be one of the greatest and most stable forces in the history of Israel. But first he had to be a little boy. And do you know how long he got to be Hannah's little boy? Three years. Hannah raised him, loved him, doted on him every second for three years, and then she obediently kept her vow.[10]

Can you even imagine what it was like for Hannah to dress her son Samuel for the last time, knowing she would never be doing it again? Think how hard that walk to Shiloh was, all twenty miles. Each step took her closer to saying an impossible goodbye. As moms, we are given a gift by God as we raise our children, for they grow slowly and we have a long time to say goodbye. Our children go from being totally dependent to completely independent in roughly eighteen years, give or take a few.

I have experienced that with my oldest son, Trevor. For both of us it has been a process of gradually allowing him more opportunity to grow and demonstrate he could be trusted and on his own. Our children, our sons not only grow emotionally but also physically. It helps a lot as we say goodbye to them when they tower over us. But that was not the case with Hannah. Her little boy was not big and he was not independent.

Innocent, small, and vulnerable, he was running off with the other children, finding bugs on the journey.

There is nothing that can prepare a mother's heart to release her small child. When they're eighteen it is hard enough. I did it recently when Trev went to college. But at three, no way. Yet Hannah did that. She walked him into Shiloh, right to the door of Eli. She told Eli this was the promised son and she was keeping her end of the vow she had made. She kissed her son, gently pushed him into the house, and turned and walked away, alone.

Wow, doesn't that just make your heart stop! You can picture her walking back over those hills alone, giving God a piece of her mind. Well, sort of. More correctly, she gave Him a piece of her heart. In fact, she gave Him all of it, she worshiped Him; incredibly, she did just that. She said God was her rock, a God who knows. She said her heart rejoices in the Lord, that He "brings death and makes alive."[11] She knew all about famine and she knew He would meet her there. Did that mean she got to run back to grab Samuel and take him home? No, it meant she could trust God with her precious son. And she could take one step after another away from him, bringing separation. For the rest of her life she would see him only once a year as she brought him a new coat.

We can learn so much from watching others endure famine. Hannah's son was not dead. What died that day was her right to raise him; Hannah died to self.

And what died that day in the classroom was not Cam; it was me. I had to die to self. I had to die to that part of me that said, "Are you kidding, God? Of course I will raise my son. Of course I will put him to bed every night. Of course I will do that until he is an adult." But I have learned that even the right to raise my son would die, and it would leave me with something I did not expect: peace and rest.

But it did not leave me without grief. Grief and peace are not mutually exclusive; they can be present at the same time. And together they can somehow bring a sense of security. It does not feel good; it feels real. It feels like you looked at the death of a dream and said, "Okay, let's do it. I don't know if I can take the first step, God, but I am willing to move." Each Friday that was what it felt like. Like grieving a death and like feeling alive.

In part, that must have been Naomi's experience during those ten years in Moab, alone with her sons in a different country. She did not have the luxury of lying in bed every day, grieving the loss of her husband. She had two sons to care for. So each day she did just that and raised those boys into men. She watched as they married sweet and lovely Moabite women, and then, tragically, she watched them both die. She stood at the graveside with her young daughters-in-law and looked at the tomb containing the men she loved. She must have wondered, *Where is God? Why did He let this happen? And what in the world am I going to do now?* At that moment she would not know it, but God had just begun to recapture her heart, and eventually she, too, would know peace. She already had the greatest tool He would ever use right beside her—Ruth.

DO YOU BELIEVE IT?

Another woman comes to mind, a woman who also once stood beside a tomb containing a man she loved, her brother Lazarus, and she was as lost and confused as Naomi. Her name was Martha and she was a close friend of Jesus. He used to stay in Bethany in the small house she shared with Mary and Lazarus. But now Lazarus was dead, and though word had been sent to Jesus that he was sick, He had not come to heal him. When Jesus came into town He went right to the graveside. He walked right up to Martha. She was not happy. In fact, she was furious.

"Where have you been? Why didn't you come? If you had been here he would not have died," she said in a voice filled with condemnation.

Would you want to move out of the way from the lightning bolt or what? Can she say that right to Jesus' face? Yes, she sure could. He was kind, He was patient, and He simply said, "Martha, your brother will rise again."[12]

Martha blew Him off as if to say, "Yeah, I know. Someday he will rise from the dead." In other words, she was saying, "That does not help me today, Jesus. I don't have my brother."

But that is not what Jesus meant. He must have turned her shoulders to Him so she could see His eyes as He said, "Martha, listen to me, look at me. I am the resurrection and the life, do you believe it?"[13] And at that He turned from her and raised Lazarus from the dead.

I wonder if you are standing outside a tomb today. What is buried in that tomb? Maybe there is a dead dream that has been gone so long that you act like you don't care anymore. Maybe your childhood is there and you are standing outside that tomb watching everyone else understand life, while you don't seem to get it. It's a dead place. Or maybe your health is there. You have suffered for so long. You are sick of even telling people how lousy you feel. Or possibly you have something God allowed in your life—an impossible situation, a famine—and it has killed even your desire and will to endure. What is in the tomb? Has a dead relationship left you bitter, depressed, and unable to move on? Has someone you loved and lost robbed you of life's enjoyment? What is in your tomb today? If God came to you outside that tomb, would you say the same thing to Him that Martha did? Would you say, "Where were you, God? If you had been here my dream would not have died. Didn't you care? Don't you know what that left me without?"

He does know, He does care, and He was there. And He would say to you the same words Martha heard, "I am the resurrection and the life; do you believe it?"

Do you? Do you believe He can breathe life back into those dead dreams? Do you believe He can revive your broken, smashed, run-over-by-a-truck heart? Do you believe it? Do you believe He can use this to recapture your heart? Do you believe that in the midst of death He can give you life that is full and abundant? He can and He is. You just have to ask Him and then listen for the answer. That is exactly what Naomi had to do as she sat in Moab. She had to listen and somehow believe that God could raise what was dead, that He could even use *death* to recapture her heart.

Chapter Three

Stuck

When she heard in Moab that the Lord had come to the aid of his people by providing food for them, Naomi and her daughters-in-law prepared to return home from there. With her two daughters-in-law she left the place where she had been living and set out on the road that would take them back to the land of Judah.

Then Naomi said to her two daughters-in-law, "Go back, each of you, to your mother's home. May the Lord show kindness to you, as you have shown to your dead and to me. May the Lord grant that each of you will find rest in the home of another husband." Then she kissed them and they wept aloud and said to her, "We will go back with you to your people."

But Naomi said, "Return home, my daughters. Why would you come with me? Am I going to have any more sons, who could become your husbands? Return home, my daughters; I am too old to have another husband. Even if I thought there was still hope for me—even if I had a husband tonight and then gave birth to sons- would you wait until they grew up? Would you remain unmarried for them? No, my daughters. It is more bitter for me than for you, because the Lord's hand has gone out against me!"[1]

SEVERAL SUMMERS AGO I learned an amazing lesson with my son Logan. On Wednesday mornings in the summertime, my boys and I periodically hosted the International Women's Group from our local university. It was the first Wednesday of the summer, and both Logan and Boone were excited to be a part of the day. The women in our group had many kids, and my boys always enjoyed being "big brothers" to children from other countries. They loved showing them how to swim, dive, and shoot each other with squirt guns.

On this Wednesday my boys were outside getting everything ready just as the women were arriving. Logan, who was about ten at the time, decided to check out the water, so he got up on the diving board and jumped. In the middle of his jump he was distracted by something and fell awkwardly, scraping his entire side on the rough edge of the board. As soon as he hit the water, I heard him cry out in pain. He swam over to the side, and I met him there. He was breathing very hard, but by the time he got to the side I could tell he was determined not to cry. He could not even talk because it hurt so badly. We sat there on the side of the pool, and I tried to help him. I asked him if he wanted to sit on the swing with me, away from everyone gathered around in concern.

But he said "No."

I asked him if he wanted to sit back in the pool with me and let the coolness of the water give him some relief.

Again he said "No."

I asked him if he wanted to go inside where I could set him up on the couch to watch television to get his mind off the pain.

For the third time he said "No."

I was running out of ideas. I knew he did not want to be by the women. It was all he could do to keep himself from crying, and he was afraid he would lose it. But I asked anyway. "Logan, do you want to come over with me and sit by the ladies and have something to eat?" He said no to this also.

Finally, after I had asked about all the options I could think of, I just sat there beside my son until his heavy breathing turned back to a calm rhythm. Soon he began to move around and eventually went back into the pool to show all the kids his very big, impressive sore. The whole episode took about twenty minutes. I did not give it much more thought. I knew Logan was okay and that for him this injury was in the past. It was just one of many such incidents I have experienced with four boys, and it was now in the category of "cool scar, with a good story attached."

I did not realize that the story was not over for me. Later that day I had the opportunity to have some time with my friend Sandy. We were talking and catching up on what was going on. I was in the middle of sorting through several big issues hitting my heart, several hitting my boys, and several involving Cameron. There were also several issues hitting my pocketbook and my schedule. In other words, there were too many things to be thinking about at once.

As I sat there in silence after telling Sandy all that was happening in my impossible life, she started talking to me. She is very practical and at moments like that she always helps me think correctly by sorting out one thing at a time. But even for Sandy this was an overwhelming task this time. Still, she was trying to help me. She kept suggesting things to me. "Becky, let's try and make of list of what you need to do first."

I told her "No."

She said, "How about some time away? Could you arrange a break time where you could go off on your own to relax?"

I said "No."

"What about going to see your counselor; she has always helped you before?"

I said "No".

She was determined. "What about getting more help for Cam? Are there any calls you can make to make that happen?"

I said "No."

It hit me after the last "no" that I was just like Logan. I was doing exactly what my son did on the side of the pool that day. Here was my friend trying to help me, making suggestions that would take away the pain, and I could not even process them because I hurt so badly. Nothing sounded good, helpful, or even possible.

I told Sandy about what happened to Logan. I told her about how I sat there beside him with all kinds of ideas about what would make him feel better, but he could not accept them. He was stuck. I was feeling exactly like Logan at that moment. I was by the side of the pool. As good as her ideas were, I could no more accept them at that moment than I could go to the moon. They sounded impossible. In fact, they were hardly reaching my brain because it felt like my heart was blocking all pathways. I was stuck. Sandy understood completely and just sat there beside me until I was calm enough to think with her.

Have you ever been stuck? Have you ever had a time when you were sitting at the pool's edge in so much pain that you didn't even know what would sound good? When others try to help you, does it sound so impossible that you push them away? Maybe you are there today. Maybe something died for you, and when you came up out of the water for air, the pain and reality of it were so overwhelming that all you could do was swim to the side and hold on. All you could do was hope, pray, and believe that somehow it would just stop hurting.

Well, if that is where you are today, sit tight. I want to talk to you a bit. I promise not to tell you what to do, but if you will listen, we might learn together how to survive by the side of the pool and allow Him to use even *this* mind-numbing, heart-searing, breathtaking pain to recapture our hearts. But in order for Him to do that, we do need to catch our breath long enough to listen to His voice as He comes to sit beside us at the pool and tell us how to get up.

As we look again at Naomi, she is in Moab. She had not chosen to go there; she had not expected to become a single mom or to bury her sons in that foreign country. But there she was, coming up out of the water to sit at the side of the pool, and all she had there with her were those two daughters-in-law who were willing to do whatever she asked. Yet she was pushing them away. It was not their fault; she was just stuck. She was in so much pain that nothing sounded possible. But at least as she sat there feeling all that pain, she had made one very important decision: she was going home.

NAOMI

There were no internet, television, or newspapers in Naomi's day, but news still traveled at a pretty fast rate. There were trade routes that ran from country to country. The traders brought not only goods, but more valuable to some, they brought news from home. Naomi had lived in Moab for ten years. I can just picture her walking to the market many days of those ten years and seeing a caravan coming through. Maybe she wandered over with her boys and asked where the men in the caravan were from. If they were from the south, her heart jumped and she asked if they had gone through Bethlehem. Each time they passed through her home town, she would ask them one question: "Is there still a famine there?" And for ten years the answer was "yes."

But then one day Naomi went to market, this time with her daughters-in-law, and when she met the caravans and asked about her hometown, there was a different answer. They told her that the famine was over. In fact, there was an abundance of bread. That day as she walked home from the market, feeling alive in a way she had not experienced for so long, she told the two young women who had been her companions in grief that she was going home.

I love Naomi. I love reading stories of people in Scripture. They give us examples of what not to do, as well as how we should act. Naomi was a cool lady. Can you see her? I picture her as somewhere on the upper side of middle-aged. She probably had quite a few wrinkles around her eyes, but not all from frowning. I see her as a woman who, despite her famines and despite the deaths she had endured, had joy and hope. In the coming chapters we will see her actions come out of that hope, even after years of famine. I think she must have been a pleasant person, because she was honest about her thoughts and feelings. People like that are great to be with. They care about what is happening, and they feel everything deeply—not only the pain but also the joy. They are the people who become passionate, dedicated fans, no matter what they support.

For years my boys and I have gone to UCLA football games at the Rose Bowl. We are crazy fans. We set up our entire fall schedule based on the games. The UCLA game is a big event, whether we are there or at home. At the stadium, we enter with thousands of other people, many clad in UCLA colors like us. Others come from work in business clothes, and some come thinking everyone is there to see them. When the game starts we are passionate about every play. Most of the people sitting around us are as into it as we are. We high-five everyone around us and generally act crazy for four quarters. If the Bruins lose the game, we feel it to the core. We walk out of the stadium really bummed. It affects the way we feel driving home and whether or not we watch the news to see the replays or even pick up the newspaper. We are serious fans. But if we win, we love it, especially if we beat USC. We hang banners and hold flags out of the windows as we drive off, yelling and clapping with other Bruin fans enjoying the win. We are fans.

But those other people who came to the game only to be with a friend or just to pass the day rarely cheered. They were more like spectators. They went to the concession stand a lot, and we had to get up every time to let them pass. They really did not care who won or lost. They left with the same level of emotion they came with. They invested nothing in the game, and they took nothing away. They didn't take away the thrill of victory or the agony of defeat. On some days after losses, I wished I could be like them and not care so much. The rest of the day would not have been ruined. But on the days we won, I always felt sorry for them, because they didn't even understand how to celebrate.

Life is a lot like those games at the stadium. There are wins and there are losses. And we are the fans. Some people pass through the seasons of their lives like those spectators. Rarely do they let anything bother them too much. They don't cheer the victories, nor do they feel the defeats. They live in control, almost on a straight line. You can't even tell whose side they are on. In fact, they often remain neutral just to protect themselves from feeling too much, especially in the midst of famine.

And then there are the fans. Now this group feels it all, is totally invested. They believe in their team and live and die with them. True fans are willing to risk caring deeply just to know that connection, to feel the joy of winning. They are willing to risk the pain that will inevitably come from the defeats of life. And as fans sit in the middle of famine, they look over almost in envy at those who keep in control. They can look at those who feel little and risk nothing and think for a moment it might just be better that way.

But that does not last long. As quickly as they catch their breath and see the tide turn, they know that they would never exchange that feeling of control for the joy of victory.

Which are you? Are you a spectator? Or are you a fan? I believe you have the capacity to feel joy in direct proportion to the pain you feel. If you are willing to go to the depths life takes you, you will know the heights like few ever do. Naomi was a fan. We see her now in the midst of loss. But stick with her as she keeps moving, and you will see something else. You will see a joy that cannot be measured as she allows God to recapture her heart.

The first step for her was to remember which team she was cheering for. She never lost sight of that. She kept asking if the famine was over, because she never gave up hope God would do something for her people. She was expectant. Even after her husband died, even after her boys died, she not only still believed there was a God out there; she believed He was working in a way that could still benefit her. So this woman, now old and weary from the losses of life, kept asking the right questions. She kept cheering for the right team. She kept listening for the right voice.

What about us? Do we have that same kind of determination? Are we willing to keep asking the right questions? Can we believe, even in the famine, that there will someday be an end to it? More than just believe, can we expect it? It takes effort to live that way. When we ask the questions, it takes a willingness to have the answer be "no," with the famine still there. That means you have to walk back home again knowing nothing will be different and not knowing when the next caravan will come through. Naomi did that for ten years. How long are we willing to trust God when the answer is "no?" Six months? Six years? A lifetime? Will you keep asking the questions, or will you just give up?

Naomi did not give up because she knew two things. First, she knew God would bless His people. Second, she knew she could always go home. She may not have known how she would do it. She might have to spend a lot of time sitting on the side of the pool feeling those losses, but she knew somehow she could go home again, even from Moab.

GOING HOME

How do we come home from Moab? Now I am not talking about the literal place; I am guessing none of us have been there. But all of us at some point have gone somewhere to escape a famine, some for an hour, some for a year, and others for a lifetime. What got us to Moab was our choices. We went after the wrong things from the wrong sources.

Moab includes stuff as seemingly harmless as raiding the fridge or as damaging as having an affair. Once you start trying to fill that hole in your heart by escaping the famine, you are headed to Moab. And what you need to know most about Moab is that God is not there. He is not in the fridge where you are trying to find something, anything, perhaps chocolate. And He most certainly is not with you as you try to find a substitute for Him in anything that will end up destroying you: chemical dependency, overspending, overeating, or overworking.

It could be looking over to another person to see if maybe they have what your spouse does not seem to give you anymore. Maybe you wonder if that other person will fill that hole in your heart, will see the need you have, will end your famine. No matter what sent you to Moab, you can know that with every step you take toward that place of escape, you are that much further away from God and His blessing. No matter how many days, weeks, or even years you have spent in Moab walking away from Him, He is still a following God. Ideally we want to follow Him because that is what being a Christian is all about. But even when we go to Moab, even when we walk away from His best for us, He still follows us.

Yet there is one thing God cannot do for you in Moab. He cannot turn you around. He cannot take that brownie out of your hand, He cannot make you stop seeing that person or stop you from taking those pills. He has given you a free will. And although He cannot physically take your shoulders and turn you around to face Him, He will be face to face with you when you do. He will walk every step back with you. Back to His blessing, back to His plan, back home.

Like Naomi, your time in Moab may not have been your choice. But regardless of who made the decision, you are far from home, and you are not sure how to get back. Before we leave Moab, the first thing we must decide is that we will listen to the right voice. After all, the wrong voice told us to leave the famine. So, like Naomi, we need to keep asking the right question. What do I do now? And the moment we hear the right answer we need to respond. We need to pack our bags, turn around, and find the road that is heading back toward home.

Maybe you have been in Moab for just a short time or maybe it has been a lifetime. If you are in that land today, will you begin listening to what God has for you to do? He will come to you, even in Moab. Even in *this* He will recapture your heart. He will go anywhere to find you.

You are never beyond His reach. And once you hear His voice, know that the road may be long and hard, but at the end will be home. The end will be the place where you can know God's blessing. It may not look the same as when you left. Going to Moab has consequences. But without question, home is always the right place to be. God is there and His blessing is there.

God's blessing always follows right choices. Just as our poor choices take us to Moab and the consequences, our right choices bring us back home, to the center of God's blessing, to the place where we can become the people God had in mind when He created us. And the wonder of it all is that in His sovereignty we are still able to be that person God intended us to be, even with our passport stamped with the country of Moab. The truth is that as you hold this book in your hands, you are the person you are today for three reasons: your own choices, the choices of someone else, and God's choices. No matter how we feel about all of those past choices, we have to agree that we are who we are because of them.

The other thing that is true of you is that you are able to make the right choice today because of the exact combination of all those previous choices in your life. Whether they were good choices or not, you can still make the right ones today. You can learn from failures, you can learn from death, you can learn from famine, and most of all, you can learn from Moab. You can still go home; you can know God's blessing.

Maybe you never left the famine. Maybe you did not go to Moab. But let me ask you, will you let someone else come back home from there? What if it is one of those people who caused a death in your life? Maybe they killed your dreams or your childhood, your hopes or your plans. Will you let them come home? Will you forgive them and free them to enjoy the blessings God has for them at home? They may not have the privilege of the same relationship with you that they had before, but they can come back from Moab. Remember, forgiveness is a choice you make, but trust is something others earn. Some people really want to come home. They really want to be different. And I have seen the blessing not only for them but also for me when I allowed someone back into my life after they had made difficult choices that scarred me. Forgiveness is not only for the people who have hurt you; forgiveness is for you as well.

Sometimes part of what death leaves us with is bitterness, resentment, and hardness of heart. Many of those emotions may be directed at someone who went to Moab, who escaped the famine instead of enduring it. What would happen if you allowed God to soften those places in you as they returned? I don't know what that looks like for you. I just know God never gives up on anyone. Coming back from Moab may have nothing to do with coming back to you. It always has to do with coming back to Him. They are never beyond where God can reach out to them. Don't make that impossible for them, no matter what they have done to hurt you. It is not easy, I know that, but maybe today you can allow them to come home—and even begin to pray that they do. Pray that even in Moab they will begin to ask the right questions and listen to the answers.

By the Side of the Pool

Naomi had her answers. She got out her old bags and dusted them off. She packed her belongings and found the road she had traveled with her family ten years ago as a young woman. But now she was without. I don't know how many steps she took before she reacted to what was happening. Maybe she went just far enough to stand on a hill overlooking the country that held so much loss for her. Maybe it was the memory of going on that road with her small boys. Possibly the young women reminded her too much of her boys, or maybe it was just feeling an overwhelming need to be alone, but Naomi reacted.

Whatever it was, she suddenly began to push away the only provision she had left, her beautiful daughters-in-law. She sat down at the side of the road, on the side of the pool, as it were, and she was stuck. Nothing sounded good, nothing made sense. Nothing and no one would suffice at that moment. She was in so much pain that there were no answers she wanted to hear. And there was no one she wanted near her.

How often we do that when we are hurting! We have made the right choices, and just like Naomi, we are heading in the right direction. We have made up our minds; we are going to be obedient. Famine or no famine, no matter how much death has left us without, we are going to do it. We are going home, following Christ. We are willing to serve

Him, worship Him, and let Him recapture our hearts. But just not right now. All we can do right now is sit here in pain.

Maybe we have been hurt so much by people or circumstances that this time we are going to do it alone. Maybe we want everyone to just wait a minute while we sit here in our loss, our grief, and our famine. We want to ask, "Can you all leave me alone while my heart and mind just can't quite function? There is too much pain and too much confusion, just too much." No matter how many good ideas are coming at us, no matter how many people are willing to go with us, all we can do is sit by the pool and hurt. We are stuck.

SARAH

What has caused you to push others away? What has left you sitting alone by the pool? What is the pain that leaves you stuck? There was another woman who was stuck. She too was sitting by the pool. She was in too much pain to move, although she wanted to go in the right direction, she wanted to believe God had a blessing for her. But it had been too many years with too much disappointment and too much pain. So as she sat by the pool, even when God came to her she did not believe He could fix it.

This woman was named Sarah. She was married to Abraham. They were *the* couple, the couple God would use to start a nation. Not just any nation, but *the* nation God would use to bless all others.[2] The only problem was that the child who was promised to them had not come. Year followed year and still there was no child, no baby. Sarah turned from a strong, healthy, beautiful young woman to a middle-aged woman who was impatient and unfulfilled. She went from that confused, unfulfilled, middle-aged woman to a disappointed and cynical old woman. She was no longer young or strong. Her long, dark hair had been replaced by coarse, gray hairs. And through all those years, she did not have a child around to renew her energy and joy. Instead, each year brought more confusion, more disappointment, and a deeper famine. She hit her forties, her sixties, and her eighties, and still there was no child. This was a dead place, and the death of her dream of having a child left her without far more than a baby. It left her without hope of ever having one. And still worse, it left her with doubt that God would ever keep His promise.

She sat by the pool not for a few minutes, but for decades. Even when God Himself came to sit beside her she did not have what she needed to believe Him. But that never matters to God. He has the power, the love, and the intention to give to us even when we are by the pool. He does this even if we don't want to listen to what He is saying to us. He can still reach in to that very stuck place and do something in us when words are not enough. That is what He did for Sarah.

There was Sarah, nearing one hundred years old, trying to keep house in a tent. Imagine being greeted each morning with the reality that you have moved another day away from the ability to fulfill the specific promise and purpose God Himself has given you. Each day likely began the same for Abraham and Sarah, alone and quiet with their thoughts.

A year earlier, uncertainty and confusion had been thrown into their lives when God came to Abraham and reaffirmed the promise He had given long before. God promised they would have a son and all nations would be blessed through that son. God was so specific. He said the child would come through Sarah. Abraham tried to give God an out, reminding Him he had a son through another woman. He wanted God to give the blessing to that child. "Why do you have to keep getting our hopes up only to dash those very hopes?" he seemed to ask. But somehow Abraham and Sarah kept moving. They kept going. They kept doing the same things they had done each day of their lives. They kept worshipping and believing, even though their hope had dwindled to the smallest corner of their hearts.

But one day everything was different. This day God came not only to Abraham, but also to Sarah. God met her by the pool. And God helped her to her feet and started her moving again. The middle of that afternoon, as Abraham sat outside his tent nestled under some huge trees, he saw three men. Immediately he knew they were no ordinary men and quickly went out to greet them. He rushed in to tell Sarah she needed to prepare the finest bread and fattest calf.

When Abraham returned to the men, one of them asked where Sarah was. Abraham told Him she was in the tent. The man replied by telling him that at this time next year Sarah would not have time to be baking; she would be caring for a baby. As Sarah heard this, she began to laugh to herself. She was by the pool. She was stuck. Even the thought of a child at her age was preposterous. She was almost one hundred years old, and she was just sick of the thought of hoping any longer. She did not want to hear one more time about that child she and Abraham were supposed to have—not from this man or any other. But this was not any man; this was the Lord. He had no intention of leaving her doubting this time. As soon as the laugh crossed her mind it was out of His lips. "Abraham, why did your wife laugh at me? Does she think anything is too hard for me? This time next year you *will* have a son."[3] And she did have a son, Isaac, whose name means "laughter."[4]

ARE YOU STUCK?

What has put you by the pool today? What has made you stuck? Has it been a long famine that has sucked the very life out of you? Has something or someone died and left you without the ability to hope, even the ability to move? God would come to you today as He did to Sarah and remind you again that what He has promised you will come true. You may laugh in His face because the years and the disappointments have brought you a deep cynicism and unbelief. Or you may even turn from Him, face the water, and kick it aimlessly with your feet. Even if you do these things, He will reach down and gently turn your face toward His. He will get your attention. He will reach past the doubt, the pain, and the loss. He will reach into that place in your heart that still wants to follow Him, that still wants to go home, and He will show you how. He will say the same thing to you that He said to Sarah, "There is nothing too hard for me."[5]

Maybe you think there is something too hard for Him today. Maybe the thing that has you stuck beside the pool feels too hard for God. It is the one place in your life that has possibly put you under the covers for another day, crying instead of living life. It is the very thing that has so paralyzed you with fear and pain that you cannot get up from that deck. *That* thing!

I know what those days feel like. Trust me, I have lived them all out over the last many years of famine. What it feels like is that life is completely on hold until God does what you think He should, would, could do for you. You agree that nothing is too hard for Him, but by the nature of your actions you are showing Him that until He acts, you will not either.

May I tell you that in that place where you are, sitting by the side of the pool, stuck, you are in the right place to experience God to the depths? If you are waiting for life to start, you are missing the point, because believe me, life is moving; you just aren't. Your life has not been put on hold as you have been stuck by the side of the pool. Your life, your dreams, your hopes are intact in more ways than you know. Because the truth for you and me is the same as it was for Naomi and Sarah. Stuck beside the pool in their lives, they learned that what they thought they wanted, what they deeply longed for, was not the bread in Bethlehem or even the promised child. What they longed for was God Himself. And the greatest lesson of the pool deck is that you learn that nothing, not even your broken dreams, not even time in Moab, can separate you from Him.

In Romans 8 Paul listed everything he could think of that might put us by the pool. Listen to him and see if any of the following have put you there: "trouble, hardship, persecution, famine, nakedness, danger, or sword." But Paul also reminds us that "Neither death nor life, angels nor demons, neither the present nor the future, nor any powers, neither height nor depth…" can separate us from His love. And just in case you have something that was not on that list, just for good measure he adds, "…nor anything else in all creation will separate us from the love of God."[6] So what is keeping you by the pool today? And what will make you get up? May I ask you, is there anyone else in your life who needs you? Maybe there is someone you don't even know who needs you to get up from that pool and go help them because they are stuck, too.

STORMÉ

I know a woman who has done just that. I met her nearly three years ago. In fact, I met her the summer I found myself by the pool. And she was one of the people who helped me get up. Her name is Stormé Sweet. She and her husband Joe came into our lives through the Aliah Sweet Fragile Hearts Foundation. They sat in my living room one Sunday afternoon and asked my boys an amazing question: "What do you wish for?"

That is an amazing question to be asked, wouldn't you agree? How many of us would love to have someone ask us that question! But as Joe and Stormé sat in my living room that day, my boys could not begin to answer their question. They were sitting by the pool and they had no idea of what was even possible.

That was no problem for Joe and Stormé. I watched them talk my boys through it and help them learn how to wish for something they never thought possible. As I watched, I just sat there thanking God for these people He had brought into our lives at just the right time. I knew little about them, but what I knew drew me to them instantly. They had come into our lives through our friends Kermit and Tami Alexander. Kermit had played with Joe in the NFL for a short time. That alone was enough to make three young boys excited, but there was more. These people had come to grant them whatever they could wish for.

Joe and Stormé had two children: Ariel, who is the same age as my oldest son Trevor, and a younger son named Aliah. Ariel is a child prodigy, singing and speaking in front of arenas before she was eight. She is beautiful, talented, and full of life. Aliah, their son, was two years younger than Ariel. From the moment he was born, Stormé knew that God had started them all on a path that would take them through a famine. And would someday, years later, put her beside the pool.

Stormé is an impressive woman. She is striking, not only physically; she is also a woman full of warmth and intelligence. She studied English through college and followed with a Masters in Film and Television. She finished her education with a law degree. She can move flawlessly and graciously through any crowd, making everyone feel a part of things. From the most wealthy and prominent celebrity to a person she casually encounters on the street corner, Stormé is comfortable with everyone and everyone is comfortable with her. If you were to meet her today you would have no idea that this captivating woman had spent over a year beside the pool.

Joe and Stormé's son Aliah was born with a rare medical condition. He was faced with multiple physical struggles and would always be in a wheelchair. He had complete receptive language, but his responses were so unique that they created a language around his verbal cues. For nearly a decade they faced challenges as a family that would grow them together as an inseparable unit. The years with Aliah were rich and deep with love and caring. So his death in the spring of 2001 left them all with broken hearts. They were left without the person God had used to teach them so much about Himself and each other. And most of all they were left without Aliah. They were left without his courage each day as he faced the unique challenges life held for him. They were left without the conversation they learned to have as he communicated with them in his own creative way. They were left with unanswered questions and with pain. And most of all, they were left beside the pool.

I asked Stormé recently what that time was like for her. She said it was a time in the depths of sadness that words could not begin to communicate. It was time held intimately between her heart and the heart of God, who met her in that place. She said she struggled in that place for nearly a year. She was functioning, yet without her heart. But as Stormé sat there, stuck beside the pool, she began to realize she was not alone. She began to look long and deeply at her talented, outgoing daughter Ariel, who was only eleven years old. She looked at what her daughter was left without by losing her brother. But she also looked at the other things she was left without, such as the many nights spent in tension and fear in the emergency room as Aliah's condition worsened. Stormé thought of what Ariel had sacrificed out of love for her brother, what life had been like for her. It was full, it was deep, but it was also different than what other girls her age experienced. Those differences had developed in her a warm and compassionate character. But it had come through pain.

Stormé began to spend more time looking at what would encourage the heart of her daughter, and slowly she began to get up from the side of the pool. Together mother and daughter looked beyond their own family and their experiences. They wondered if there were others with special needs children and the challenges they bring, people who were still stuck by the pool, and with no answers. With Joe they began the Aliah Sweet Fragile Hearts Foundation in the spring of 2002.

The foundation's purpose was to grant wishes to siblings of severely handicapped children. Their website perfectly describes the heart of the foundation and the deep understanding their family has for the unique needs these families face.

The Aliah Sweet Fragile Hearts Foundation provides respite to siblings of severely disabled children with life-threatening conditions. The focus of a family with a child having serious medical conditions is often out of necessity on the disabled child. As a result, familial interaction and balance can be delicate. Many of these children have complex feelings of extreme love and guilt. Understandably, they desire the full attention of their parents, but they also appreciate the extraordinary needs of their handicapped brother or sister. The Aliah Sweet Fragile Hearts Foundation is an organization that focuses on the sibling. It enriches the lives of siblings by granting their wishes and special requests.[7]

Six years and many wishes later, we had the privilege of meeting Stormé and Joe. Stormé is no longer sitting by the pool. Now she is sitting in living rooms like ours. She is facing children who have forgotten how to wish. Some have had so much taken from them that they have forgotten how to ask for their dreams. There are few dreams left in them. In fact, Stormé says often the only wish these children can come up with is the one impossible to grant—that their sibling will be healthy, just like them, so they can play and talk together.

I watched as Joe and Stormé sat patiently with my own sons, looking at their answers on the application and gently prodding them to think bigger. "What do you really like, Boone?" I heard her ask my son. "If you could have anything, what would it be?" I never could have asked him that question. But here were these amazing people sitting in my living room, helping my boys learn how to ask again. They were helping them get up from the side of the pool.

My boys' wishes were as varied as they themselves are. The first wish to be granted was for Boone. He had asked for a video game player. That, of course, was not a big enough wish for Stormé and Joe to hear. Stormé' noticed Boone was a sharp dresser and asked him if he might like a shopping spree at his favorite store along with the game device. Boone's eyes shone, which they took for his "yes." They made all the arrangements at his favorite shop in town.

The store opened an hour early on a Saturday morning. The other boys and I drove Boone to the shop with a blindfold on so he would not know where we were going. We fumbled with maps and feigned entrances to the freeway just to get him there with a sense of surprise. We were all laughing by the time Joe, Stormé, and Ariel met us in the front of the store. They stood there with a gift bag brightly decorated with balloons and containing his game player as well as a coupon for a shopping spree in the store. As we walked in, the manager added several more gifts to Boone's growing pile and ushered him into an empty store set up just for him. As Stormé and I talked, Boone ran up to us to show off a new watch he was considering. "It's $200 though, Mom," he said, and for the first time in my life I heard myself say, "No problem son, you can afford it!" Within an hour his shopping was done and all our goodbyes were said. We left for home with a carload of treasures from the store and my son beaming. Without question, his heart had been recaptured!

Logan's wish was the simplest of all. He wanted blinds for the large front window of his room because it took in the hot afternoon sun. This wish, of course, was too modest to be acceptable, but it gave Storme' at least a starting point to work with. She said, "What if we redid your entire room, Logan?"

He said, "Sure, that would be great!"

His furniture was old, a mixture of nursery stuff and some of Trev's hand-me-downs. She told Logan to expect a call from her design team in several weeks. The call came from a wonderful woman who lived in Mission Viejo. Together with her friend she came out and met Logan and talked to him about his interests. She found out he loved two things: football and UCLA. The room would be built around those two concepts. The only requirement she made was that we have all the furniture out by the day they came; she and her team would take care of the rest.

Logan was gone the weekend they arrived, which allowed plenty of time and space for Joe and Stormé and the twenty or so volunteers we had in our house that day. They built all new furniture for him, including a brand-new desk and chair. Two new dressers matched the desk. He also had a new bunk bed with completely new bedding, all of it matching the colors and football theme. But that was not all. A dark green rug with yardage lines and numbers stenciled on it covered the floor. There was also a huge UCLA rug on the wall between brightly painted yellow field goal posts. They even put a steel plate on his wall to act as a scoreboard for any football games played on the floor.

For Logan's windows, the gal that designed the room went online and found several football plays and drew them out on three sets of pull-down shades. The finishing touches came the next week, when Logan was visited by several members of the UCLA football program, including two of his favorite players. They had a signed jersey and football for him from their Sun Bowl victory the previous season. Needless to say, my son Logan was no longer by the side of the pool; he was hopeful, he was encouraged, he was moving!

My oldest son, Trevor, wanted to see the Pac-10 tournament final at Staples Center in the spring of that year. As the tournament arrived, it was clear that UCLA had a great shot at playing in the final game. Trevor was allowed one guest and chose his cousin Corbin, who shared his love for both UCLA and basketball. They sat together with Joe in the front row, right on the floor at Staples center, where both the Lakers and Clippers play their home games. They watched UCLA win the tournament in seats that typically would be filled with Hollywood stars for an NBA game. Trevor received a signed jersey and basketball from the team that went on to play in the Final Four that year.

The boys loved having their wishes met. They enjoyed their gifts completely. But more than having the wish granted, what they loved most was realizing their dreams with Joe and Stormé themselves participating. They were there for every wish. They even treated our whole family to a UCLA basketball game where my boys were allowed to meet and talk with the players after the game.

Stormé and I sat in the upper deck watching the game. But what we enjoyed even more than the game was watching my boys with Joe, all of them sitting in the student section on the floor. Joe was having as much fun as the boys were. While I sat there with this amazing woman, I was so grateful not only to God for bringing her into my life, but also to her for having the courage to face the famine. She was able to see what death had left her without and got up from the side of the pool to lend a hand to the rest of us who were just plain stuck.

Are you stuck today? How long have you been sitting beside the pool, kicking aimlessly at the water? How long have you been watching the ripples move out from you in that perfect circle, wondering if life will ever make sense to you again? Have you, like Naomi, said aloud, or even only thought, "It has been harder for me than for any of you. You would not understand. Just leave me alone in my pain."

Let me tell you, He understands. He comes to you by the side of the pool and tells you, like He did Sarah, that nothing is too hard for Him. He asks you as He asked Stormé, "Will you look around from this place and see if there is anyone else beside this pool you might be able to help?" Or maybe He would simply say, as He did to Naomi, "You are heading in the right direction. You are going home. You are almost there; just get up and keep walking. But as you do, don't push away the provision I have for you. In fact, sitting by the pool with you is the person I will use most powerfully to recapture your heart. Her name is Ruth."

Chapter Four

Determined

At this they wept again. Then Orpah kissed her mother-in-law good-by, but Ruth clung to her. "Look," said Naomi, "your sister-in-law is going back to her people and her gods. Go back with her."

But Ruth replied, "Don't urge me to leave you or to turn back from you. Where you go I will go, and where you stay I will stay. Your people will be my people and your God my God. Where you die I will die, and there I will be buried. May the Lord deal with me, be it ever so severely, if anything but death separates you and me." When Naomi realized that Ruth was determined to go with her, she stopped urging her.[1]

THEY CAN'T TOUCH YOU

I GREW UP in Southern California. Since my high school days, I was aware that one of our local amusement parks transformed itself completely for Halloween. I have never had a desire to go to the Halloween version of that park because frankly, I hate being scared. I had reached adulthood perfectly content to know that I would never experience this adventure unique to October and that I would simply enjoy the park the other eleven months of the year. That was until the fall of 2006. My oldest son, Trevor, was a very trustworthy seventeen-year-old, and one cool autumn Friday night, he had gone with a group of his friends from church to experience the park. He came home absolutely beside himself, adamant that we had to go with him the following Sunday.

Let me continue to paint this picture so you get the full experience. The following Sunday evening he was talking about was a night before school, for one thing. It also just happened to be the opening Sunday of our brand new fifty-acre church facility. While the rest of the staff went home exhausted after the long hours required to open our facility, I began to gear up to go out to a very scary park with Trevor and my two younger sons Logan and Boone, who were, of course, thrilled to be out this late on a school night.

The park did not even open until late in the evening. This should have been a huge red flag to me. Another concern hit me when we got in line and I quickly saw I was the oldest person there. But my three sons could hardly contain themselves, which in and of itself was enough to put my tired body in line with a bunch of adolescents at an amusement park at ten P.M. I love having fun with my boys, but as the line inched forward it began to hit me that we would soon be in the park, exposed to a bunch of people who had been hired for the express purpose of scaring me to death.

Trevor had counseled us the entire forty-five minute drive about how to act once we got inside the park. It was like a game, and the perception of fear was the key. He told us there would be "monsters" on rides as well as walking around and in the mazes they had constructed all over the park. These monsters would be actors dressed up in costumes and masks. They would be wearing special gloves with metal pieces on them to make a lot of noise. But the most important thing Trev told us, and he told it to us many times, was that THEY COULD NOT TOUCH US. The whole idea is that they make lots of noise, wear scary stuff, and jump out from dark corners just to scare us, but they are not allowed to make contact in any way. Trev coached us the whole drive about how to act in the middle of mazes as the monsters surrounded us. He said to just keep walking, follow him through the maze, and not to act scared. As soon as the monster senses you are afraid, he will follow you all the way through, and you will never get rid of him.

Sounds like lots of fun, huh! Well, I had no idea as I entered the park that night that I was about to experience one of my most fun and memorable nights with my guys, as well as learn a powerful, life-changing lesson. We entered the first maze soon after we walked into the park. Trev said it was a good "starting maze." Not too scary, just fun.

Well, as we waited in line to enter the maze I saw quickly what Trev defined as "fun." There were several monsters waiting around the lines, sporadically jumping in front of someone who looked a little nervous. As I stood there, I wondered how not to look nervous. We navigated the line, made it to the entrance of the maze, and walked into what seemed like a super-amplified haunted house. There were lots of props, tons of music, and monsters around every corner. Trev took the lead, which was reassuring to all of us. He was imposing, a big, athletic guy whose very appearance would tend to keep the monsters away from him, but most important, he had been through all the mazes before and knew what to expect.

So there we were, inching our way forward as our line of people zigzagged through the maze of neon lights, morbid sights, and big, hideous guys popping out of the walls. As we moved ahead, Trev was leading, with Logan right behind him, followed by Boone; I was in the back of our little group. To say I was uneasy is an understatement. I tried to muster up that old confidence I had learned as an athlete but could not find it. This was in every way my worst nightmare, and it was just beginning. And this was the "easy maze!" *What am I going to do when they really get scary?* I asked myself, as I somehow made my feet take each step toward the dark corners that held unknown horrors.

I am not sure when it happened, but somehow toward the end of that maze, as the fake fog and lights began to dull my vision, I made a decision. I grabbed the back of Boone's shirt and decided I could do this. I would walk through that maze behind my son and let those monsters think I was not afraid, that I was helping him through the maze, and that they might as well leave us alone. Boone was braver than I was, but holding on tight to him somehow gave me the courage to face the monsters around every corner. When they jumped out at me I began to give them that look that all mothers know. The one that says, "Come on, you think that scares me? You have to do better than that; I am a mom, after all. I have laundry piles bigger than you!" So that is what I did. I kept a death grip on Boone's shirt and defied those monsters to even try to scare me.

By the time I exited that first maze, my adrenaline was through the roof. I was ready for more. "Where is the next maze, Trev?" I had this place down. I learned the secret. No matter how afraid I was of these monsters, no matter what means my mind could conjure up that they might use to try to paralyze me with fear, the truth was more powerful. THEY COULD NOT TOUCH ME.

So as we progressed through each maze, we boldly followed Trev. He would deftly turn corners, looking back at us and pointing out the monsters lurking there. Logan followed bravely behind him, Boone came next with the same courage, and I kept right with my boys. Boone could barely breathe because of the way I was pulling his shirt, but I was right there with them, facing my worst fear as we went around each corner. I looked it in the eye saying, "No, you can't scare me; I know the truth. You cannot touch me, and even if you could, I think I could probably take you out." As a matter of fact, I gained so much confidence that on the last maze there was this little werewolf-looking monster that kept going after Logan. He was getting ridiculous by the end of the maze because he would not leave Logan alone. So as we were exiting, I sent the boys ahead with Trev, and I cornered that little monster, stuck my finger in front of his fake snout, and told him to leave my kid alone. I am built like a middle linebacker, and the guy was pretty small, so mask and all, he took off running. It was awesome!

MONSTERS

What a night! What a lesson. As I finally drove home in the early morning with my three sons sound asleep, I thought about all I had just experienced. I thought about the many places in my life that make me afraid. I thought about the truth I know from God's Word, that nothing can defeat me. It was as if that night in the car God was saying the same thing to me that Trev had said earlier. THEY CAN'T TOUCH YOU.

Sure, the enemy can take many forms in my life, can come at me in many ways. And like the monsters in the park, they can make lots of noise and take on some pretty scary forms. Everything from mounting bills to the rising number on the bathroom scale, from air conditioners that need fixing to cars that won't start, from hearing an impossible diagnosis to opening the mail to find divorce papers—all of them monsters.

But as I drove home that cool fall night, I began to learn an important truth. There are many things that will make noise, distract me, even put me by the side of the pool, but if I am able to look at those things for what they really are and can shake my head at them like I did at those monsters in the park, I can say, "Right, do you think you can really do this to me? Do you know who I am, or better yet, do you know who my Father is? He is the Creator of the universe, and He will take you out if you as much as touch a hair on my head. You cannot touch me, you have no power over me, and I am going to just keep walking right past you sorry excuse for a monster." You know what that is called? Determination

That kind of determination is built on the truth that nothing can really harm you when you are trusting in God. I did not learn determination in those mazes based on what I could do to those monsters. In fact, I was holding onto Boone for dear life. No, my determination was based on the truth that no matter how afraid they made me, those monsters could not touch me. The same is true in life when we take a hold of the truth that no matter the sound or shape the monsters take, we have a God who is bigger, a God who can be trusted. That makes us determined.

Determination means looking at my life, monsters and all, and seeing things for what they are—and more often for what they aren't. I can't close my eyes and still expect to make my way through the maze of life. In the same way, if I continue to let my fear overwhelm me, I will keep stopping, keep cowering in the same corners and letting those same old monsters swarm over me. I need to have determination. I need to have the courage to say "No, I know the truth, and the truth has set me free." And I am just going to keep walking in the right direction and trust my Leader who already knows the way. I am going to look at the maze of my life for what it is, and then I am going to hold onto Him with all my strength and somehow keep walking. I don't know about you, but that is exactly the definition of my day-to-day existence. This journey scares me to death, often overwhelms me, and almost daily exhausts me.

But I am determined to keep walking in the right direction, holding on for dear life.

Don't you just love it when God puts someone there for us to grab onto? I can remember distinctly how much strength I felt when I grabbed a chunk of Boone's shirt in my hand and held on. It became such a joke to the other boys, but my little Boone understood. He was so sweet. Each time we entered a maze he slowed down until he felt my hand grab him, and then we walked on.

What are you holding onto today? I don't have to know you to know you have plenty of monsters making noise in your life. Who do you have that will slow down for you? Who will just wait until he or she feels your hand take hold of their's and then will walk with you through the maze of life? What a treasure those people are. God is so good to give them to us. He often uses our family and our friends to remind us of the promises we hold onto. That is exactly what Ruth did for Naomi. She slowed down and let the tired, bitter, sad old woman grab hold of her cloak and walk with her on the long, hard journey home.

ORPAH'S CHOICE

Let's take a second to remember where we left our gals. They were up on a hillside somewhere, looking over Moab, and Naomi was pleading with her two young daughters-in-law to go back home and leave her alone. The girls did not want to leave her. They both obviously loved her and wanted to help her. They were selfless and kind young women. And on that hillside they both faced a choice that would set the course for their futures.

The first to respond was Orpah. She made what appeared to be a hard choice at that moment, a choice that required her to separate herself from Naomi and from Ruth. To move away from the new life she had known with her husband and this family from another land, people who worshipped another God. She had known pain but also, I am sure, great joy in this family. Leaving would be hard, but it would also be safe to go back to what she had known. We never hear from Orpah again. That does not mean she turned out bad or did something terribly wrong. No, like Elimelich, she made the logical choice. She did what many of us would do in that situation. She responded to what was happening in front of her based on what she knew was safe. It was just another choice in a life full of choices, but this choice cost her so much because it did not include the living God. Naomi said it so clearly as she turned to Ruth while Orpah walked away. She said, "Go with her, Ruth, go back home, go back to your gods."[2]

Those words must have hung in the quiet, still air. Orpah was making a choice to walk away from all the blessings and provision from the living God that Ruth would know. She would not be used by God to touch the lives of millions of people. Her words would not be recorded, cross-stitched on wall-hangings, written in songs, and quoted over and over like Ruth's. Her name would not be in the middle of the genealogy of the Messiah. Orpah would not be an example of determination. She did not make the hard choice. In retrospect, she made the choice many of us make. The easy one. The one that takes the pain away. The choice that in one sweeping move will seemingly solve all our problems. However, we don't see on the front side of those choices how many other problems we have created, or most of all, how many opportunities we have missed.

We are faced with those kinds of choices all the time. We can choose safety or we can choose risk. To put it in other terms, we can choose to live by sight or we can live by faith. As Orpah stood there, overlooking her hometown and her country, the most natural response was to go back to what she knew, to what she could see. Even a quick glimpse down the road to Bethlehem showed that route to look a little bleak.

First of all you had Naomi, and bless her heart, but she was not the most engaging company, nor did she seem to want Orpah around. Then you had the long, hot, tiring journey full of potential dangers for three single women, and afterward you had the new country to deal with. She would be a foreigner, poor, an alien, an outsider. Who would blame her for going back? Nothing about the option of going with Naomi seemed very inviting, nothing you could see, nothing obvious. That is, unless you were willing to see what was not there. Willing to believe God could create something out of nothing. That you were sure that the one thing you would not miss in your life is living in the middle of the presence of God, no matter where that took you.

ABRAHAM'S CHOICE

Abraham had that choice. God came to him at a time when he was pretty well set up in his hometown. He was wealthy, had a good-looking wife, and the respect of his neighbors. He probably had a pretty nice set-up. He was living out the "American Dream," except that he was doing it in the land of Ur. God gave him a choice. He could keep living that way or he could pick up and move somewhere else. The catch was that "somewhere else" was a little vague. In fact, God's exact words were that He would lead him to "a land I will show you."[3]

That is saying a lot, coming from God, the Creator of the universe. He could have meant the moon for all Abraham knew. So he faced a choice. He could do the safe thing and stay in the place he knew, or he could follow this God who seemed worth giving up everything for. He made the hard choice, the risky one. How was he rewarded? Did he get a bigger house, more land, a huge family with many children and grandchildren to comfort him in his old age? Did he get to retire in some nice climate and look back over a life well lived? Kind of, but not the way we would envision it.

That is usually the way God works. The reality for Abraham was that he would wander in this new land God would show him. He would go from place to place, always living in a tent. He would wait many years before he had that promised child. And the only piece of land he would ever own was the one he would be buried in beside his wife. At the end of his life God told him he would have a huge family and that they would someday settle in the "promised land." But that would not happen until years later, after hundreds of years of slavery.[4]

Wow, that really makes you want to make the hard choice, doesn't it? But you can't define the choice simply by its outcome any more than you can define the hope you hold onto on the way. When you choose obedience to what God asks, He is in charge of the results. He measures them and He blesses them. And He is the only One that matters. What He said about Abraham was pretty amazing. He called Abraham His friend. How would you like to be the friend of God? Not an acquaintance, but a close friend. Someone who not only trusts God, but someone whom God can trust. That trust did not come easily; it came through obedience and it came through determination. It came by making the hard choices, the right choices.

YOUR CHOICE

Maybe you are facing a choice today. Are you overlooking some familiar territory, faced with a choice of leaving it behind for something that seems a little crazy? Maybe the very people you have trusted are telling you not to go, not to risk it. They are the people who stand outside the park and say, "Becky, come on, don't you see you are the oldest one here? Aren't you tired? You have had a long week. Why don't you just go home. Besides, there are MONSTERS in there. You are not the kind of person who likes to be scared. It's not your thing." All of those statements are true. In fact I used them myself as I waited in line, but had I made that choice, I would have missed so much.

What are you in danger of missing if you choose the "safe" thing, make the "reasonable" decision, the choice that factors in only what you can see, what you know, what you can offer?

What if you make another decision as you stand there, overlooking those two paths? What if you look at both options and, like Abraham, turn to God and say, "I will go with You even if that means I will never have a house, never have a place to call my own. Even if I have to wait for the promise, even if I never see it in my lifetime, I will follow You."

Is He worth that to you? Is He worth following even if He takes you far from what you know? Even if He takes you on a journey you did not expect, on a rough, steep road filled at times with monsters? Will you choose to go anyway? Will you choose the eternal thing, the impossible thing, the risky thing? Will you choose to hold on for dear life? Will you make Ruth's choice?

RUTH'S CHOICE

Ruth. Now there is some woman. I have always loved Ruth. Before I could read, I remember being told her story by my Sunday school teachers from one of those cool Bible story books. Those books had very few pictures in them. The best part was getting to the stories that did have pictures, and Ruth's story always had one. It usually showed her picking up barley at the harvest. I remember that she looked very beautiful, very exotic. She had lots of jewelry on in the pictures. That seemed strange, since it looked like she was doing yard work at the time. But most of all, even as a young girl my impression of her was that she looked like a strong woman. A woman who was sure of herself and most of all, a woman I wanted to be like when I grew up.

You know, as I look back, there are few better biblical examples to emulate than Ruth. She did it right, and she did it so flawlessly that, as we look at her picture in those old storybooks, we could easily forget she was a real living and breathing woman full of hopes, dreams, and emotions. When we look at those we most admire, we forget at times that they had to make hard choices, too. They wanted to go back home as much as we do. That is what Ruth faced as she watched her sister-in-law walk back down the hillside toward home. She had to choose something else, something she could not see. And she had to choose it through pain.

As we look at those two women left standing alone, the only ones remaining in that large family, we could easily forget that they are both widows. Not only had Naomi lost a husband; Ruth had as well, and she faced a long life of uncertainty. And for all she knew, as she made her decision and turned away from the only home she had ever known, she was also turning away from any hope of having a family of her own. She was going to Israel, where she would be a stranger, a foreigner, an alien. In Moab she would have had parents, probably brothers and sisters, too. As she turned toward Bethlehem she only had this woman beside her, a woman who had made it clear she did not want anyone around.

Despite all that, however, Ruth spoke those unforgettable words. She not only said them; she meant them. She literally turned on her heels and headed in a different direction toward an uncertain future. Can you hear the determination in her words? Listen to them: "Don't urge me to leave you or to turn back from you. Where you go I will go, and where you stay I will stay. Your people will be my people and your God my God. Where you die I will die, and there I will be buried. May the Lord deal with me, be it ever so severely, if anything but death separates you and me."[5]

Don't you just love Ruth? What does it do to you when you read that? What does it do to your heart, your hopes, your dreams? That kind of stuff really gets me. It makes me feel like doing something for someone. It makes me want to go through my overstuffed drawers and closets and give everything away. It makes me want to go help someone, give to someone, encourage someone.

What it does not allow me to do is to feel sorry for myself. Too bad, huh? No pity parties on the hillside overlooking Moab, only hard, clear, determined choices. The kind of choices that lead you to a life full of meaning, hope, and purpose. The kind of life that allows you to think of others first, mostly of God, and all around, less of yourself. It was the kind of choice Boone made every time we entered one of those mazes. He was scared too, but he slowed down just long enough for me to grab hold of his shirt. In that moment, in that split second when his mind switched from his own fears to mine, he made a choice to help me.

That is the choice Ruth made. Sure, she had plenty of pain in her own heart. She had heard all that Naomi had said to her about staying. She had watched her sister-in-law leave. But at that moment the most important thing to her was not her own comfort; it was Naomi's. The deciding factor was not what she wanted, but what God wanted. Why could she make that hard choice? Why could she do the right thing on the hillside that day? Because Ruth had a really good teacher, Naomi.

A Good Teacher

Naomi, that tired old woman standing next to Ruth on the dusty road out of Moab, the one who was working so hard at pushing her away, had been her teacher. There was no other way a young woman from a pagan country would give up everything to follow a God, any god, unless she had been taught some amazing things about Him. It was not only love for Naomi that kept Ruth on that hillside; it was faith. It was a powerful belief in a God who could do something from nothing, change hearts, and bring healing—a God who somehow, even in the midst of terrible loss, would have a plan for her.

That is the God Naomi must have shown Ruth day after day in Moab—the one true God, the living God, the creator God. The God who would someday send a Messiah, a deliverer for His people. Naomi would not in her wildest dreams have imagined that the young woman who did the laundry beside her and helped her with meals would actually be in the line of that Messiah. Or that the Deliverer who was coming would save not just the people of Israel, but all people. Naomi did not know how big His plan was or how intimately she would be connected to it, but she knew enough to share with Ruth about this God who was worth giving everything for.

I wonder where she started. Do you think she sat Ruth and Orpah down and taught them the language of her people? Did she get to the Hebrew word "Yahweh," look seriously at both of the young women, and tell them, "That is the name of our God. He is not like any other god. He is the God who made the heavens and the earth"? All of that from a single mom raising her sons alone. Powerful testimony, a great teacher. Naomi was real, her needs and desires were real, her pain was real, and most of all her faith was real, and it must have been contagious.

Somehow, in all that time, Naomi had communicated a very big and real God who was even more powerful than Ruth might have imagined. A God who cares and who delivers His people. A God who would deliver her. Naomi might have told Ruth and Orpah about how He had parted the Red Sea for the Israelites when they came out of exile. Or maybe while they were cooking a meal she told them about how God made food fall from heaven each day for His people while they wandered in the desert. I do not know which stories she told, but I know she told them something, because when everyone else would bolt, Ruth found a reason to stay. She alone had faith and the determination to stay with her mother-in-law and her mother-in-law's God. In fact, she had enough determination to slow down and allow Naomi to grab hold of her to take the journey.

What a gift. It must have been shocking for Naomi to hear those words of loyalty and commitment come out of her young daughter-in-law. Those words and the power behind them silenced her and allowed her to simply turn around, grab onto this amazing young woman, and start walking home. And with each step, she was beginning to learn how to face those monsters of pain, bitterness, and loss that had been making so much noise in her weary heart for so very long.

DETERMINED ACCEPTANCE

So if it was determination Ruth showed on the hillside that day as she turned toward Israel, how do we find that same steadfast resolve as we face the choices in our lives? Determination is all about choices. The One who gave us the free will to make those choices has some pretty good advice for us. Listen to what God has to say about the choices we need to make. "Today I set before you life and death, blessings and curses, *now choose life.*"[6] (italics mine) Those are great words, and all of us would say that we agree with God, that our desire is to choose life over death. That seems obvious, but the challenge consists in moving what we desire to do into action and beginning to make choices that bring life.

I believe our choice must begin with acceptance. Acceptance is a great word. Its definition alone encourages strength and determination. It is defined in terms such as a willingness to believe something is true, coming to terms with something, the act of willingly taking a gift. We would probably all agree and accept those definitions.

But let's move out of the English classroom and apply those definitions to our lives. Not just any part of your life, mind you, but the most challenging part, the loudest monster, the most heart-rending and painful part of your lives. How much determination and strength do you feel now? How willing are you to accept that monster? How willing are you to look at that hurtful place, whatever it is, as a gift? How are you doing in coming to terms with it? And most of all, how willing are you to believe the truth of who God is, even when those monsters are making noise all over your life? That is exactly what Ruth did on that hillside, and that is what we must do in our lives to find the determination to make impossible choices, to choose life today, tomorrow, and for the rest of our days.

But before we can choose that way, we must begin by accepting life for what it is. In order to do that, you have to affirm two things about your life, no matter how wrong it feels to be in the midst of that struggle, that famine, no matter how big the monster you face is. First, there is no one to blame for this pain, and second, you are okay even if it's impossible to fix, because maybe, just maybe, it does not need fixing; maybe it is right.

NO ONE TO BLAME

We live in a society of victims. If this means there is at least one villain per victim, there are a lot of bad guys out there! We have learned that if we are in pain there must be someone to blame for it. We have grown up with the cartoons and animated movies which clearly had a good guy and a bad guy. There was no question as to who was wrong and who was right.

As you well know, life does not allow us those clear lines. In our minds we might make them, but if our actions continue to reflect that we are victimized, we are more likely to make Orpah's choice than Ruth's when we stand on the hillsides of our lives. In that case, each time we see those monsters, we cower, because we take them as villains who will overpower us. Determined acceptance begins in your mind, by thinking correctly about your life. Does that mean no one hurts us? No, people will hurt us, and unfortunately, we will hurt others until the day we die. But we are not victims; we are not powerless to overcome the pain we are in. And we do not have to find someone to blame just because we are hurting. Often life just plain hurts.

One of the most amazing gifts God has given me in the process of raising my son Cameron, was the freedom He allowed my heart to experience in the midst of all the struggles. I accepted all the pain, all the burden of what his life means, without having to add to that pain by desperately finding someone or something to point my finger at. By God's grace, I did not blame the medical profession or the school district. I did not fight the diagnosis, and I did not become consumed with making it right. I accepted it. Acceptance is not passive. In the case of raising Cam, acceptance could not have been more active. Although your body is busy, it is possible for your heart and your mind to have peace.

I want to be very clear. I was never okay with the struggles; I do not like any part of how Cam has to live. It is hard and often painful, but I have not tried to blame someone for the pain we are in regarding Cam, and I have not looked down every rabbit trail to find a way to get us out of it.

My oldest son Trevor is now in college several states away. The fall of his freshman year he called to tell me about the interview he had had for his new job. It was with the mother of a severely handicapped boy. After getting the job, Trevor picked him up from school and stayed with him several afternoons a week. I was so proud of him, I was so thankful he would choose to surround himself again with disability, even after leaving his home that held such unrest because of it. I was thankful he wanted to give to this family. And most of all, I was grateful to God for the ability He had given me to rest in a few places of my heart. Somehow, in the midst of a ridiculous life I had created a home where, although there was chaos, there was also calm. And somehow, underneath all the pain there was a place to stop. A place to rest. There was stability. Life would always be undone, but somehow it was not wrong.

You may not have a child with severe disabilities, but I am certain you have experienced pain in your life. And I am learning that pain is pain, no matter the source. It drives you to do things you would not otherwise want to do. It makes you panic; it can crush you and overwhelm you to a point where you are sure you cannot hold up under it unless something changes. It is the famine we talked about in Chapter 1. It is real, it is hurtful, and sometimes it is permanent.

What are you going to do with that pain you feel today? Will you sit in it and find some measure of peace by pointing a weary finger in the direction of someone else? That is not peace; that is vengeance, and it can feel good for a minute. After that minute is gone, however, vengeance will only add to your pain. You could also take that pain, throw it over your shoulder, and begin a desperate search to get rid of it, to somehow make it better or go away. That path will only allow the pain to consume you even more. Or you could take that pain out, look at it long and hard, and say to it through narrowed eyes and clenched teeth, "You cannot touch me." And live your life in determined acceptance.

My son Cameron is a beautiful boy. Yet spending more than two minutes with my family will show anyone how different he is from other children. If at any point in the last eleven years since Cam was diagnosed, God had decided to touch his life and make him just like his brothers, I would have thought that was amazing. I would have praised Him and worshipped Him.

But that kind of miracle is not required. It's not like there is nothing to heal. There is something; Cam is severely disabled. However, he is not wrong. He is, I believe, exactly as God allowed him to be. There was no mistake. There was no accident, no one to blame. I live in a sinful world filled with disease. My job is to accept the fact that God has the right to use any part of this fallen world to recapture my heart. He is in control; He makes choices. Even if that involves allowing autism, cancer, death, and disability. I am not powerless or helpless; I can look at the places in my life that won't change, and I can see beyond the pain to what God is doing.

You may be sitting there right now, shaking your head. You may be angry with me for writing that. You may have lived your life on a crusade to blame others for your pain or to find a cure for it. Please stay with me, please keep reading. This is what I most want you to hear.

I know how much pain hurts, I know it is hard, and I am sorry it feels like this. But you can go deeper than the pain to what it is ripping out your heart, you can grab that peace back, and say "No, you can't have this, too." Pain can absolutely destroy us, but it does not have to. That is not what God intended for it to do. He intended for it to heal us, to make us whole. He planned to use that pain to recapture your heart and mine.

If we believed He was behind that pain, when we are hurting we would have to say that He is the last person we would trust with our hearts. If He is responsible for the awful hurt, why would we want Him? I will tell you why. Because He is bigger than the pain. He is worthy of the heart-wrenching journey we take when we grab hold of that tether of pain that emanates from our hearts and follow it all the way back to Him. What you find when you grab that cord and hand-over-hand follow it all the way back to the heart of God, is that He is holding the other end, not in His hands, but right in His heart. You will find something better than a cure; you will find understanding. You will be given a greater gift than someone to blame; you will see a God worthy of worship.

APPLYING THE LESSON

Do you have any places in your life that include pain? I am talking about a brutal, want-to-hide-under-your-covers kind of pain. What are you doing with it? Are you blaming someone else for it? Do you know that as your pain grows, so will your villain? Are you ready for that? Do you want a bad guy the size of King Kong to try to forgive? If you allow people to be the right size in your mind, they are easier to handle in your heart.

How big are the people you are blaming for your pain? How consumed are you with them? Do you know that those people you carry in your heart with bitterness and anguish often don't even give you a second thought? All that time, all that energy is going toward those thoughts circling in your mind and heart that never get out, and while in there they can do some major damage. So if you have a "King Kong" sized bad guy out there somewhere, forgive, let that person shrink back down to size, and get on with your life.

Maybe you don't have a "King Kong" monster out there, outside of you. Maybe the monster you have created to blame is you yourself. You have lived with the regret and pain of failure for many years. You are consumed with it, and as great as you feel the pain to be, you feel the guilt of your failure even more. Go to God with your pain. I am guessing that if you have felt it for that long, you have probably confessed your guilt hundreds of times already. You don't have to tell Him you are sorry again. Tell Him you are done carrying it and leave it at His feet. It is a monster that may not be able to touch you, but the fear you have lived with has made that monster chase you around for years. You have been cowering in a corner, afraid someone will find you out.

Well, God did. God knew everything you would ever do before you took your first breath. He looked it all over—the darkest points, the secrets, and the shame. He put it all together and gently laid it on the broad, bruised, and bleeding shoulders of His Son. He died for the sins of the entire world. But you know that, don't you? And still you carry it, as if He could not be bothered with your awful sin when He has so many others to deal with. That is not true. That is a lie. The truth is "if we confess our sins He is faithful to forgive us our sin and cleanse us from all unrighteousness."[7] All.

No matter your monster today, no matter who you have chosen to blame for your pain, you can stop. You can let all those monsters go back to normal size. You can let out the breath you have been holding and exhale, rest, relax. Living life that includes pain is hard enough without all those monsters chasing you around. They can't touch you, but they can be annoying or worse if you let them stay around. Chase them away and start living, now. Not when your pain goes away, but now. Not when you are cured; do it now. Not when you finally find the man of your dreams, but now. Not when you have the baby you have always wanted; start living now. You are complete, you are whole, and you are forgiven. Now be content.

We are living in a fallen world, so contentment is not a given; it is a choice. Contentment is not based on your circumstances; it is based on your choices. It takes determined acceptance. It is not easy. But how much fun has it been for you to live with that pain coupled with guilt and bitterness? Let it go, exchange it all for the greatest gift God could ever give you—His peace.

Ruth knew that peace as she moved along that long, dusty road back to Israel. As she walked beside Naomi, I am sure she thought long and hard about what she had experienced over the last few years of her young life. Ruth was not looking around for someone to blame. She accepted that there were some pretty hard places in her life. She acknowledged there was pain that may not go away. She did not try to cure her pain by running back to Moab, looking for a husband to cover the hurt and hopelessness she felt. No, she demonstrated determined acceptance. And as she walked, I can imagine a tired Naomi grabbing onto the back of her cloak for reassurance, for hope, and for the strength she would need to go home.

HOLDING ON

Ruth demonstrated determined acceptance as she turned with Naomi toward Israel. Naomi also showed determination as she grabbed onto this young woman and headed home. It is hard to go home again after your life has fallen apart. At times home is the hardest place to be when you are hurting, but it is often the right place. For Naomi home represented more than just the provision of food; it was walking back toward all she knew. Home was where she would find her people, her family, her customs, her language, and most of all, her God. But before she could experience her old life, she had a long journey ahead of her. She needed determination. She needed to hold on.

When we think about determination, most of us come up with images of powerful people doing great things through their own strength, through some deep kind of steadfastness that helped them through something impossible. I like to define determination as holding onto something more powerful than you. Over and over in the book of Hebrews the writer tells the weary, discouraged people to "hold on."[8] He does not tell them to try harder, do it all better, and ignore the pain. No, he simply says they can't touch you, so hold on.

Now the truth was that the writer's audience was being touched, some of its members in very harsh and even deadly ways. But the writer of Hebrews did not promise a quick cure; he said they cannot touch what is eternal. The Message Bible says it this way: "Keep a firm grip on the promises that keep us going."[9] This is where determination gets really interesting. It is less about changing your circumstances and more about holding on as you move through them. But if we are honest, I think we would all have to say that when life gets hard we want to bolt. We want to close our eyes and ball up in the corner. We want to go under our covers and have a good, long cry. All of us have done those kinds of things in one way or another, and each time we do, we can picture those monsters swarming all over us. Our fear has made us helpless against them.

So what would it take to be determined in the face of our monsters? How do we keep holding on in the midst of our long journey home? Let's start where most of us get into trouble, in our minds.

MIND

The Bible has a lot to say about the capability of our minds. "We have the mind of Christ,"[10] so we can even think the very thoughts of God.[11] As fantastic as that truth sounds, the one that catches my imagination is a command to take every thought captive. There is something amazing about that concept.

Studies show we have about ten thoughts per second, and that adds up to 36,000 thoughts per hour and a whopping 500,000 per day. We even have over 30,000 thoughts while we are sleeping. Now how in the world do we take a half million or so thoughts captive every single day?[12] And how do we begin to set their direction in order to help us hold on in determined obedience?

Women are known to speak quite a few words. I am as guilty as any other woman of the sheer enjoyment of hearing the sound of my voice. But as many words as I use each day, the truth is that I have thousands of thoughts that never make it out of my mouth. But those thoughts don't just sit there in my mind; they get busy, and the outcome of all that thinking has a huge effect not only on my words, but on my actions and choices each day. So how do you focus those thousands of thoughts and move them into the direction of determined acceptance in order to help you hold on to the truth and move in the direction God desires?

You have to be very intentional. You have to be careful what you put in. I remember when I walked into the student lounge at Biola University for the first time my freshmen year. Beside a large television there was a plaque on the wall that read "Finally, brothers, whatever is true, whatever is noble, whatever is right, whatever is pure, whatever is lovely, whatever is admirable—if anything is excellent or praiseworthy—think about such things."[13] That was a not-so-subtle hint to help us understand the types of things we should and should not be watching. But more important than what we allow ourselves to see is what we allow to filter into our minds, what we allow ourselves to think about. Paul began with the essential, the key component to focused thinking; we are to begin by thinking about truth. How many of the 500,000 thoughts that circled in your head last night were true? How many were noble? How many were pure, lovely, admirable, praiseworthy, or even right? What an amazing passage to use as a measure for our thoughts.

You must know that before a single word came out of Ruth's mouth on the hillside that day, she had to make up her mind as to what was true, noble, and right. Before I took another step forward in one of those spooky mazes, my mind had to win a battle for the truth I had heard over and over from my son. However frequently those monsters stopped me in my tracks, the truth was, "They cannot touch me." I knew that was more true than the convincing threats they were making.

What battles are you fighting in your mind right now? In the midst of that barrage of thoughts, are there any true thoughts fighting to be heard? Or are those thoughts simply pushed aside, as fear, frustration, and failure win out? The negative voice always seems to be the loudest one we hear.

Many people have been told all of their lives that they would amount to nothing. They were not beautiful, they were not talented, they had no worth or value. Possibly you have heard some such words. They are not true, but the problem is that even though those voices are silenced, the words have turned into nasty thoughts that swirl around in your head and are still heard. Instead of that unkind person's voice, the only voice there now is yours; you have taken up that negative voice as those defeating kinds of words swirl around in your own mind. The sad part is that you are taking it all as truth. It is not truth. It is a monster, it is a lie, and it cannot touch you. But first you must see it correctly for what it is, and that is where your eyes come in.

EYES

I do not have good vision. I have not been able to see the "E" on the chart for many years. The last time I had to do the eye test to get my driver's license, my children, who were then toddlers, stood beside me and tried to give me the answers out loud. It was pretty bad. But more recently, when I went to the eye doctor she said some amazing words. She told me my eyes had improved. I was shocked. I was used to my prescription always getting slightly stronger, but this time my doctor told me that the good news about being forty is that your eyes begin to give up and give in, responding to the correction instead of fighting it. In other words, my eyes finally got the message that they could not see very well and started adapting to those little round things I had been shoving into them for the last thirty years.

I wonder how long it takes our eyes to give in to the realities of what they see in our lives. I wonder how long we fight the view that is there, never accepting what life has held for us. Just as my severely myopic eyes fought those contacts, we fight off any help available for us to see our lives clearly. But if we do not see what is there, we will never be able to develop the kind of determination we need to accept it.

So what have you and I missed all these years? At the top of the list might be our own ability to fail, to see clearly and understand honestly what we have not been able to do. Face it. Accept it. Even embrace it. Talk about a monster! Our failures can be impossible to face up to. I believe I would rather live with failure than face it. I would rather believe I will lose those forty pounds, write down another list and make a new plan to do it, instead of facing the fact that I have been unable, unwilling, or unmotivated to do it for several years now. I must accept that fact.

The greatest benefit of accepting those failures is that you are then dealing with the truth, with reality, not with what you believe it is or should be or would be if you would just do things better. Out of the ten or twenty places in my life I have been given to see more correctly over the last years, God has allowed me to change some of them, while others are still under review. My problem for all these years has been my looking at ten or twenty areas at the same time and presuming they should all be great. But just as my eyes gave in to the help my contacts had offered and responded with greater vision, so also did my heart and mind as they began to accept the reality I am beginning to see in my life today.

The pleasant part of seeing ourselves and our circumstances in this new way is that we can now see some things in a softer, more realistic manner. We can make choices about what to change and how long it will take. We often take years to practice doing something wrong but give ourselves only days to improve. It may be more realistic to believe that what we see can change if it needs to, but probably over time. This view would literally be a sight for sore eyes!

MOUTH

We have talked about how to hold on with determined acceptance as we think and look at the circumstances surrounding our lives. Now comes an even harder part. A significant tool God can use is our mouths. Our words speak literally volumes about who we are and what we are doing. They can condemn others as well as ourselves, but our words can also encourage, challenge, and affirm.

The Bible has lots to say about how we use our words; it is very clear on the subject. "Do not let any unwholesome talk come out of your mouths, but only what is helpful for building others up according to their needs, that it may benefit those who listen."[14] So it is not just about what you don't say; it also is about what you do say. We need to be proactive with our words, constantly looking for a way to encourage someone, especially if that person is yourself.

God has been very specific as to how we use our words regarding others. We are not to gossip. We are not to slander or even speak true things about people that others do not need to know. We are not to spread rumors, even as "prayer requests." Basically, we are not to use our words to cause trouble. We all know how dangerous they can be when directed at another person, but I believe the greater danger is how we use words in relation to ourselves.

The way we talk about ourselves is very important. First of all, we should not talk too much about ourselves. I know I am in the pit when I look at a ranting email to a friend and I can trace the letter "I" several times in every sentence. That means "I" am the subject way too often.

We have many opportunities to use our words to encourage others on their journey as we hold on with determined obedience. A sure way to struggle in our own lives is to take every opportunity to cut ourselves down. To do that is not helpful, it is not funny, and it is not even comfortable for others to hear. But for some reason we think we can have this open monologue of destructive words running unhindered from our own lips. Words that damage, words that hurt us, words we would not want others to say, yet somehow we allow ourselves to say them.

I teach several hundred women on Thursday mornings. They have loved and supported me through the most challenging times of my life. As I have taught them these last ten years, I have learned from them the things I should and should not say. Overwhelmingly, the one thing never tolerated by them is that I say something negative about myself. Even a passing joke at my own expense falls like a brick in the silent room. Those women love me and they would not allow anyone, not even me, to say things like that about me. Their silence has spoken volumes. I have learned that it is not kind, it is not sensitive, and most of all, it is not necessary to use unkind words about myself. They are not funny; they are hurtful. They affirm negative thoughts that run through our minds. To allow such a thought to stay long enough in our minds to form into a word is very damaging. To speak that word, to hear that word out loud is incredibly destructive to our spirits. Words can hurt. They can hurt others and they can damage us, making it almost impossible to hold on. We need to use our words to encourage ourselves and others. The words that come out of our mouths must build up and encourage our hearts.

HEART

Our hearts! Where do we begin to look at our hearts? Our hearts so often get us into trouble, but at the same time they create the most wonderful experiences of our lives. God will do anything to recapture our hearts. They must be recaptured for two reasons. First, because they are His; He alone has ownership. And second, because they are the place where we most often wander from Him.

Our hearts are the seat of emotion; they are where we feel. That can be a double-edged sword, because our feelings can and often do take us away from truth, from the things we have set our minds on. If we make choices based purely on our hearts, they can often be wrong. If we live our life based only on our feelings, they can betray us and cause us to do things we should not. We may feel things that are untrue and at times destructive. When we struggle to accept ourselves and others, we find it impossible to be determined, and we let go of the truth. We cower in front of monsters that cannot touch us—all because of the way we feel.

But as much as our hearts can get us into trouble, without question they are the organs that most clearly reflect and glorify God, if we have His heart. If we care for those things He cares about, just watch out, because when our hearts are right there is no end to our determination.

I have made a standing request to God for His heart. I want to care for what He cares for, to feel for people the way He does. Not only for other people, but even for me. I am still in the elementary stages of that process. But I am certain it is the right prayer. I am also certain that the answer to that prayer comes in the form of determined acceptance. Nothing drives me more than my heart. My heart leads me directly to action. I feel deeply, and because I feel deeply, it makes me want to do something. That is not always possible, and at times it can be frustrating. But when my mind, my eyes, and my mouth are all in order, my heart really fuels them to hold on.

It is a risky prayer to ask for God's heart. He may require action toward people you are not accustomed to even noticing, let alone helping. If you ask for God's heart, He will allow it to break for the lost and hurting and for those who cannot help themselves. For the unloved, unwanted, and under-resourced in your city and in the world. But the great part is, He will use you to recapture their hearts. He will use your heart, alive and beating in rhythm with His, to reach others who are hurting. The amazing part is that all of a sudden your heart feels whole. It is not dragging behind you; it is out front, leading you to those people you can love with His love.

HANDS

Our hands seem to be the most vital tools we have for holding on. They are critically important not just for what they hold onto, but also for what they are willing to release. As much effort as we think we may be exerting in holding on, a ton more effort needs to be applied to letting go.

It is not easy to let go of things in our lives. There was a reason we took hold of them in the first place; they are important to us. But as long as we are holding onto those people and places, we cannot possibly hold onto Him. We don't just drop those things, of course; we place them in God's hands.

I remember when Cam was a very little guy. He used to play with rocks in the backyard. He walked up and down the grass, looking for small rocks and picking them up. It did not take long before he had so many rocks in his hand that each additional one dislodged another and it fell to the ground.

I watched him for a while and then offered a solution. I said, "Cam, bring the rocks over to me and I will hold them." This was not something Cam immediately wanted to do. He was protective of his little treasures.

Finally I walked over to him and carefully helped him dump the rocks into my cupped hands. The great part was that Cam now had unlimited space for new rocks. He began again to search for them, each time bringing them over and dropping them into my hands. This worked well for a while. However, he eventually got a little anxious about those rocks; he kept looking at them each time he dropped a new one in. So after some time he walked over to me, reached in with both hands, grabbed out as many rocks as he could, and began that same previous process of addition and subtraction.

When we look at the things in our hands, we can be like Cam at times. We really love the treasures there. Most of them God has handed to us at some point. But the more we add to our lives, the more full our hands become and the more apt we are to drop some of those precious treasures on the ground. We carefully try not to do that, but the reality is that we can do only so much.

We have so much freedom when we take those precious treasures, those people, those opportunities, those dreams, lay them in the hands of God and leave them there. One at a time, we can drop them into the place of ultimate safety. Our hands are now free, wide open to hold onto Him with determination. But just like my fearful son, we look over at that growing pile in God's hands and think, *Wow, maybe I should be doing something with some of those places. I wonder if God needs my help here?* And we take back handfuls from Him to again carry the weight and burden of responsibilities we were never designed to take on.

What are you holding in your hands today? Are you so busy adding to that pile that you have not even noticed that rocks have been falling out the other side? We are good at holding parts that relate to other people, but those things can take up space for our own needs, such as rest, exercise, and sleep. What has fallen from your hands as you have tried to add more to what you are doing?

We need to release all those places to Him, all the circumstances, all the people. Other people, just like us, also need to have open hands to hold fast to Him. As much as we believe we are helping others by holding onto them, the truth is, only God can hold them. All we need to do is leave them in His hands and hold on tight.

FEET

We are holding on. We are determined. Our mind is focused. We have taken those many thoughts captive. Our eyes are seeing life correctly. Our mouth is speaking truth, speaking kindly not only to others but to ourselves. Our hearts are beating in the same rhythm as God's; we feel what He is feeling. Our hands are empty, simply grasping tightly to Him. And to add to all of that determination, we need to keep our feet moving in the right direction.

The journey through the famines of our lives is a long, winding, steep climb. Our feet play an important part in this journey. They keep us moving. You cannot have determination when you stop moving in the direction to which God has called you. Ruth and Naomi never would have seen the promises God had for them if their feet had not taken them back home to Bethlehem. We do not have to move fast; we just need to keep moving. Many times in this journey it is all we can do to put one foot in front of the other, to take just one step forward. But like in those mazes at the amusement park, if I do not keep walking, the monsters will pounce. So as I think correctly, look at my life with 20/20 vision, speak the truth, have the right heart, and hold fast to Him, I must do it all as I shuffle along toward home, my feet willing my body to keep going.

WILL

I spent about an hour not long ago at the eye doctor with my son Boone. Unfortunately, he seems to have inherited some of my poor eyesight. For several years now he has worn glasses. I say that in the most generous sense. The truth is that for these last five years Boone has had his glasses in front of his eyes for only a few months total, since we have a hard time holding onto things made of wire around here. Cameron loves to manipulate anything metal, and more times than not, Boone's glasses have ended up in some amazing design on the floor. We made a decision the last time he was at the doctor to consider contact lenses, and finally this week we went in and tried out his first pair. As we drove to the office I gave Boone my two cents about this new journey.

Once we got there, after some encouragement and some effort on Boone's part, the doctor put contacts in his eyes. He loved the way they allowed him to see without glasses. He loved that he could look normal and not have to squint to see across the room. He was excited.

But now came the fun part. The lady helping us brought us into a tiny room that had only a counter and shelves and shelves of contact lenses. On the counter were a mirror and an assortment of solutions to put on your lenses. She handed Boone an empty case and instructed him how to take his lenses out. After several tries and a process that looked to me like he was taking his whole eye out, the lenses somehow landed in the correct case. Victory! "Now," the very patient and calm woman said, "Boone, I want you to put them back in before you go home."

What sounded like a simple request turned, for Boone, into an hour-long battle. Well over a hundred times in those sixty minutes I watched my son pick up that tiny bluish piece of plastic, perfectly balance it on the top of his index finger, gingerly put a tiny drop of solution on it, and try to pry his eye open to shove it into place. Each time the lens fell back onto the counter or folded over on his finger, Boone took a deep breath and started the whole process again. Finally he got the lens in his right eye. However, this was a short-lived victory, because he soon realized that it was in backwards and had to come back out. Though he had not won a total victory, his partial success allowed him to move on to the left eye, where he continued the same process as before—patiently picking up the lens, inspecting it to make sure it was correctly on his finger, adding one drop of solution, and lifting it up to his eye. Each time the lens dropped he let out a disappointed breath, as the very kind woman and I looked on, silently encouraging him with each failed attempt.

As I watched my son's shoulders fall each time he saw that lens on the counter I thanked God for this time of character forming He was allowing him to experience. It was frustrating to the core for Boone, but he was determined to get those lenses in his eyes. He knew he would not be able to leave that office until he put them in. So every single time the lens slid off his finger he put it back in place and tried again.

Finally, on one of his many attempts he blinked the lens into place, and he was done! We left the office quietly, and he sat in the car and put his seat belt on without saying a word. He was exhausted. As we drove home I told him how proud I was of his determination, while he sat there, eyes red from constantly being poked at, one lens in his eye and one in his case. The words from Mom could only go so deep. What was deeper in his heart was the reality that putting those lenses in was really hard, and tomorrow he would have to do it again.

Life can feel a lot like those long afternoons at the eye doctor. Like my son, we can try to do the same thing over and over, experiencing little success or progress. We can leave those exhausting times of our lives feeling little victory, as we sit there with one contact lens in and the other perhaps backwards in our painful, bloodshot eyes. And just like my son, the only way to move through those times is to exercise determination in the form of our will.

Our will is the sum total of all the other parts we have talked about. Our minds and eyes, our mouths, hearts, hands, and feet all work together at the direction of our will. Our will is the place where we make decisions. It is what made Boone keep putting that lens on the top of his finger. It is what moves us through the mazes of our lives, past the loud monsters. It is what keeps us holding on when everything is screaming at us to give up.

When life is challenging enough to pull you out of all your normal abilities to cope, when you can no longer see, feel, or keep moving, your will is what holds you. We all know those moments are exhausting, and we often feel hopeless, driving home, as it were, with only one contact lens in place after a major battle at the doctor's office. But we need the will to keep moving. It was her will that allowed Ruth to make the hard choice on the hillside overlooking Moab. It was Naomi's will that drove her to take hold of her daughter-in-law and begin a long journey home.

We all have wills. We all have a place in our guts that makes the hard decisions when the rest of us wimps out. We simply need to exercise it. Like all other exercise, it is a process. We do not desire and do the right thing automatically or even correctly the first time. But as we make those gut-wrenching decisions, we have to know the same two things my son knew that day in the doctor's office. We must know that first, we cannot move on until this is accomplished, and second, every time we do it right it will get easier. When you are sure of those two things, your will is ready to move your feet, raise your hands, direct your heart, form your words, and focus your eyes, and most of all, fix your thoughts on the next thing needed to hold on.

MICHELLE

I met Michelle for the first time one Thursday morning after I had taught our women's Bible study. She introduced herself to me and asked if we could get together and talk sometime. We arranged for an afternoon she and her two children could come to my house. As we sat in the backyard and she told me her story, I was amazed at the journey God had walked this young woman through.

When you look at Michelle you see a woman with many of the same qualities I am certain Ruth possessed. She is tall, beautiful, her complexion is dark, and everything about her movement denotes strength, purpose, and determination. Michelle is a single mother. She is in her early thirties and has two children. Her daughter Tori is eleven. Tori is tall like her mother and has many of the same outgoing qualities. Her son Ethan is seven and is as busy and active as he is tall and wiry.

Michelle began her story with her sophomore year in high school. It was the year she met Matthew, who was tall, dark, and very handsome. They dated all throughout high school and married in 1993, soon after they graduated. Michelle was eighteen and Matthew was nineteen. They moved to Riverside, joined a church, and settled into a home. They had the typical dreams of young married couples. They looked forward to having children, taking vacations, growing old and gray together.

They welcomed Tori into their home several years later, and life was very good. In the spring of 2000, Matthew had a great job and Michelle was an at-home mom raising a busy toddler and five months pregnant with their son Ethan. But then, on what seemed like a normal morning in May, life changed forever for Michelle. She opened the door to see a man from her husband's company telling her that Matthew had died in a tragic accident at work. Her 6'7" husband had suffocated underground as he tried to do some electrical work.

Michelle was stunned. She moved through the next few days with the help of family and friends. She sat there night after night, trying to make her mind work, her eyes focus, her mouth speak words of comfort to her tiny daughter. She tried to get her hands and feet to move her through the days and tried to get her heart to somehow start working again, not only for her benefit, but also for the new life inside of her. It did not happen automatically, but slowly, as all the people left her to go back to their lives and silence filled moments that used to contain laughter and lively conversation. Slowly Michelle's will took over. She opened the pages of her Bible and found this promise from God: "So do not fear, for I am with you; do not be dismayed, for I am your God. I will strengthen you and help you; I will uphold you with my righteous right hand."[15]

Over the last eight years Michelle has experienced God's strength, she has felt His right hand upholding her, and she has known His presence. Does that mean life is easy? No. But life is good. She made a decision to trust God, to fix her will on what she needed to do. Just like Ruth on the hillside that day, this beautiful young widow made a choice and began her journey home. A journey that would take Michelle, like her ancient counterpart, far away from the monsters and right to the center of God's incredible blessing.

HANDS IN OUR POCKETS

We had had such a great time on our adventure with the monsters that my boys and I decided that our October trip to the amusement park would have to become a yearly tradition. So as the anniversary of our first visit came nearer, we booked a flight for Trev to come home and again lead us through the mazes.

But this time it was different. As we drove to the park, we did so with a car full of my boys' friends, some of whom had never been there. It was so much fun to hear my little guys sharing their exploits of the year before. Once we entered the park, everything was different there as well. We were veterans and our confidence showed it. I no longer held Boone's shirt, and Trev no longer had to lead us through the mazes. In fact, Logan took on that role for most of our dark journey through the monsters.

There was one particular maze at the far corner of the park, however, that Logan was not looking forward to; this one was filled with monstrous clowns. Clowns are just creepy, in my opinion. Logan did not like them either and was very willing to skip the maze altogether. But the rest of our party really wanted to go, so he gave in. As we waited in line, Logan moved toward the back of our group, and I could tell he was not very excited about what the next few minutes would hold. But just as we were about to walk into this particular maze, he brushed past Trev and all his college friends, thrust his hands in his pockets, and led us through that maze without even a pause. I walked behind him, amazed at his poise and resolve in the midst of some pretty determined clowns. But not a single one made him hesitate. When we reached the end of the maze, I asked Logan how he did it, how he had walked through that maze so fearlessly.

He told me that he knew they could not touch him, but he wanted them to know that he knew. In other words, when he put his hands in his pockets he was telling those monstrous clowns "I know you can't touch me, but I want you to know that I know. I am so not afraid of you that I won't even try to block you; I will just walk right through the maze as if you were not even there." That is determination.

Are you willing to do that in your life? Do you know that those monsters can't touch you? Are you so sure of that fact that you will actually shove your hands in your pockets, as it were, and walk through life full of confidence, no matter the monsters?

When we do that, we are saying that we do not need to defend ourselves against the monsters that challenge us. We do not have to put our guard up. Like my son, we can be vulnerable and yet unafraid. I love that. I want to live like that. I want to be that determined. Just like my son, just like Ruth, who on the hillside overlooking her home country turned with her weary mother-in-law, stuck her hands in her pockets, and made a very long journey.

How about you? What choices are your facing today? What monsters are staring you down? THEY CAN'T TOUCH YOU! Will you believe that firmly enough to keep walking? Will you know that truth well enough today to stick your hands in your pockets and take the next step? You may know it, but will you show it? Will you, like my son, demonstrate with your actions that you want those monsters to know that you know? That no matter what they do, no matter what noises they make, you will live a lifetime of determination.

Part II

The Harvest

Chapter Five

Honesty

~

So the two women went on until they came to Bethlehem. When they arrived in Bethlehem, the whole town was stirred because of them, and the women exclaimed, "Can this be Naomi?"

"Don't call me Naomi," she told them. "Call me Mara, because the Almighty has made my life very bitter. I went away full, but the Lord has brought me back empty. Why call me Naomi? The Lord has afflicted me; the Almighty has brought misfortune upon me."

So Naomi returned from Moab accompanied by Ruth the Moabitess, her daughter-in-law, arriving in Bethlehem as the barley harvest was beginning.[1]

IMPOSSIBLE PAIN

I SAT IN silence in the large classroom at my son's junior high school. Logan had invited me to hear him speak at his Navigators Christian Club meeting one afternoon the end of February, 2008. I myself have spoken to this group, but this time, instead of filling the role of a guest speaker, I sat marveling at the composure and insight demonstrated by my tall, blond, thirteen-year-old son. He had grown so much in the last year, physically as well as emotionally and spiritually. The long, gangly arms now fell from broadening shoulders, and the dark blue eyes that usually darted around nervously were now set and focused on his classmates as he spoke with them that afternoon. He had chosen to speak on the passage in Matthew about the temptation of Christ in the wilderness.[2] He had done a great job preparing his talk; he had even given it to me out loud several times as we ran errands the days before. As he reached the end of his presentation that day, I waited, praying silently for him, as I knew the depth of the words he was about to share with his friends. Words that came from an impossibly soft heart that had had to deal with an impossible set of circumstances that very week.

Several weeks before the day of the talk, Cameron had a violent outburst in the car. The episode was not uncommon for us, but the fact that it took place in our car and was directed at Boone was unusual. The outcome of this incident was several large and deep scratches across Boone's face. Within days of that incident in the car, authorities became more deeply involved in our case, and previous events were looked at with greater concern. The result was a permanent placement for Cameron in residential care. I cannot actually type those words these many months later without it causing my heart to stop. The thing our family had both most needed and feared was about to become a reality.

It took several weeks until all the necessary funding and paperwork were in place. The date for Cam's move was set for exactly two days before Logan's talk at school.

The morning Cam was to leave our home for the last time is one that is so deeply etched in my mind and heart that I will always be able to tell you the color of the grass that day and nearly how many leaves were beginning to form on the bare winter trees that lined our street. The boys and I walked Cam to the school van that had picked him up in front of our house for years. We all hugged him and said hushed goodbyes to him. As the van drove away with Cam inside, the three of us stood on the curb and held each other and cried for a very long time. We knew what Cam would never understand. When later in the day he arrived at the group home where he used to stay for respite, he would find his unique, boat-shaped bed and the rest of his bedroom furniture from home. In some way peculiar to his mind and spirit, Cam would know that something had greatly changed in his world, and he would process that in his very simple heart.

The boys and I knew another very hard reality: he would be doing it alone, since we would not be seeing him for a month as he began to transition into his new home. As we turned back toward our house, the "For Rent" sign was another brutal reminder of the changes that were being thrust upon us, as nearly half our income was from the state and was now going with Cam to provide for his care. My boys would pack up their belongings and leave the only home they had ever known. They soon would give many of their things away as we moved into a house exactly half the size of the one we walked back into that day.

My mind and heart were filled with the fresh memory of that scene as Logan reached the conclusion of his talk. He discussed how seventh and eighth graders could find application to their lives in Jesus' temptation in the wilderness. I heard Logan list some things that might tempt them as junior highers. Moving from the general to the specific and deeply personal, I saw tears in his blue eyes as he began to try to describe to his close friends what life felt like to him in the last emotional days and weeks before Cam's placement. He told them how he and Boone were not twins, but rather triplets, and that the brother his classmates had never seen or heard much about was named Cameron. Although Cam was nearly as big and certainly as strong as his brothers, his mind was like that of a baby. Logan told his friends how it looked when Cam was upset and throwing a tantrum and how violent he could be. He told them about his recent outburst and its outcome: Cam would now need to live in another house.

Then my tall, handsome son told them how it felt to say goodbye to Cam for the last time. Even deeper than the description Logan gave was his depiction of what all those emotions tempted him to feel: lost, angry, hopeless, bitter, scared. As Logan traced his talk backward and reminded them of Jesus' reaction to temptation, he talked about some of the ways God had walked him through those honest and deep emotions. Many of the students were in tears as they listened to powerful words from a very real boy who had lived a real life of famine. Logan could stand up in front of his friends and speak the truth that day for two reasons. He knew he could always be honest with the God who made him, and he knew he had a home that would always be a safe place.

HOME

A home is an important part of the culture of any family. In recent years, as we lived in our home in Southern California, we have learned that a home is not only a place of value, but a place to be protected, loved, and at times, rebuilt. Southern California has endured drought conditions for many years in a row. The drought, combined with the varied terrain of our region, has created "perfect storm" conditions for fires.

About mid-October, warm winds stir in the deserts and blow westward across Southern California communities beautifully nestled in hillsides. The fires can be ignited by lightning, downed power lines, careless ashes left burning in a campfire, and sadly, even by the hand of an arsonist. Regardless of the source of the fire, the outcome is always the same, tragedy. The losses from our fires in the fall of 2007 were staggering. The evacuation of homes necessitated by those fires caused the largest people movement in the history of our country. The final number of lost dwellings reached into the thousands. As a result, thousands of families drove back into charred neighborhoods, turning each corner in hopes their homes would still be standing. As families walked aimlessly through the remains of what had been their homes, their response was invariably the same: grief and dismay. The charred pieces they sifted through were more than the walls and framing that used to surround them; they were all tiny parts of what made that place their home, and now it was gone.

The families affected by the Southern California fires of 2007 will rebuild houses that were lost. Once those new structures are up, they will move in, and only then will they try to recreate the home they grieved in its charred remains.

A home is so many things. It is shelter. It is security. A home can be a refuge, a haven. What a home should always be is a safe place. One of the most amazing things my counselor told me to do with my boys after my divorce was to tell them often, in fact all the time, these simple words: "You will always have a home with me."

So I began to say it, dutifully at first, even if I tacked it onto a sentence that had nothing whatsoever to do with home. But as the years passed, that statement became a staple in our vocabulary. So much so that when

I began to say it, my sons immediately finished my sentence. I would say "Just remember, Logan," and he would quickly add, "Yes, Mom, I know; I will always have a home with you."

It was not until one night several years later that I really understood what I had been saying to them all those times. I was putting Boone to bed, and as I began to leave the room and turn off the light he said, "Mom, remember you will always have a home with me." It was cute, it made me smile, then it made me think. What I had done on all those occasions is define what "home" meant for my boys. Because I had consistently used that phrase at all different kinds of times, my boys had learned that home was where you were most yourself. On any given day that might be goofy, thoughtful, angry, or silly. All those emotions were contained in our home. Home was a safe place.

That does not mean it is a calm, quiet, or even peaceful place. My home is none of those things. It is where my boys go to figure out life. The most consistent prayer I have made for them is that they would have soft hearts, and they do. But the reality of soft hearts is that when you put a group of them together, it creates a loud place. Because soft hearts feel, they feel joy to the heights and pain to the depths, and both often cause a loud response. But the roof of my home has yet to come off. All of it has been contained; it has been a safe place.

That night, when Boone turned the tables on me and used my own words to encourage me, there was more to learn than how the guys had come to define the word home. That night I believe God was saying to my heart, "Becky, remember, you will always have a home with me." That would mean that just as my boys had the freedom to experience life to its fullest in front of me, I also had that same freedom to live my life out loud in front of God. He wanted the goofy stuff, the intense things. He would listen to the whining, the silly jokes, and the loud cries and tears. He was my home. He could contain it. He was the only One who could. What an encouragement that was to me that night. What a thought—God is our home. He is a safe place. And in that safety I have felt the freedom to be honest with God in recent years as the direction of our lives took turn after turn that I did not want, expect, or like.

One of the many shocking revelations I had that spring of Cam's placement was the truth that although I had told Logan, Boone, and

Trev hundreds of times that they would have a home with me, I had never directed those words to Cam, because they were not true in his case. That reality never occurred to me until I began to process that he would no longer be living with us. Home was no longer a safe place for Cam, and there was nothing at all okay in my heart with the truth of that statement.

NAOMI'S HOMECOMING

Naomi was way ahead of me. She had long understood that God was her home. In fact, she was on a journey right back to the heart of where He would bless her. Naomi knew that as her home, God was ready, capable, and most of all willing to let her live life out loud right in front of Him. As she walked back into town she was very serious, very angry, and very hurt, and she was more than willing to let everyone, including God Himself, know it. As we will see, she does not mince words; she is very clear and very direct. And amazingly, there is no lightning bolt that follows her words—only silence and understanding.

That is what you find when you go home; that is what you get when you finally unleash your pain, fear, and disappointment at the right place, at the right time. It is relief. It is called honesty. God is not offended by it, and ultimately, when we direct our honesty to the right place, there is not only healing, but there is a real kind of magnetic presence. Naomi was the kind of person who said what others only had the audacity to think. She had courage, conviction, and an audience. Her audience was not only her old friends, but God Himself.

Naomi had left Bethlehem as a wife and mom of a busy family of boys. She left with hopes and dreams wound up and intertwined in the lives of those three men, the three most important people in her life. She left with the desire, as all moms have, to provide more than just meals and clean clothes, but a truly safe and healthy place for her boys to grow up. She was truly full as she walked away from Bethlehem. As she walked back, however, she made one incorrect statement: she said she was empty. She was in fact full, but all the longing that had filled her as she walked away from Bethlehem was now replaced with pain.

Listen to her words as she nearly spit them out after her long, hot, difficult journey home. "Don't call me Naomi," she told them. "Call me Mara, because the Almighty has made my life very bitter. I went away full, but the Lord has brought me back empty. Why call me Naomi? The Lord has afflicted me; the Almighty has brought misfortune upon me."[3]

Naomi is clear in her thinking, she is clear as to how she feels, and most of all, she is clear in who is responsible. Her statement is true, because it is not about her; it is about God. And whether you are praising or railing, when your words are about God you are starting at the right place. Because everything is truly about Him, even those things that affect you. And the fastest way to really know the fullness that Naomi found so illusive is to start and end with God.

JOB'S WORSHIP

One of the most ancient stories of the Bible is still one of the most applicable in times of famine: the book of Job. My friend Sandy and I reserved it for one of the last books to study, partly because we were afraid God would use it for some heavy application to what we were living out, and after all, who wants to invite suffering? But when our time to study that book finally came around, it was an amazing experience and a lesson in true worship.

Job is a fascinating story. In the first few chapters we see heaven "unzipped," and we are allowed to look into this little drama between God and Satan playing out up there. We see this remarkably casual kind of interchange that includes talk of a human named Job. Job makes heaven's conversation not because he is misbehaving, but instead because he is doing everything right. God looks down, spots Job, and says to Satan, "Have you seen this guy? He is amazing, look at how well he is doing."

Satan's response is, "Sure, who wouldn't do well if he had as much as Job has." Satan insists that if he could have his way with Job and remove some of the things that are good in his life, Job would then, like the rest of humanity, fall apart and curse God. So God allows the attempt.

Wow, that kind of grabs your heart, doesn't it? That God would seemingly go along with a plan that Satan appears to originate? But you have to stay with the story. This plan is all about God, His glory, His love, His desire to bless, and His ability to be sovereign. So Satan is allowed access to Job, and he takes and takes.

Talk about moving from full to empty. In one day all of Job's family and wealth are gone—everything. He tears his clothes, shaves his head, and falls to the ground, grieving and mourning losses that cannot even be counted or measured. But in the middle of that grief, in the middle of the deepest famine he has ever known, his response is that he came to the world with nothing and will leave with nothing. And for all of that, God's name is to be praised.

Again we see heaven unzip and witness another conversation between God and Satan. This time the outcome of their discussion is that Satan will be allowed to take Job's health away.

The response from Job is sharp and immediate and again very clear. He sits in ashes and laments the tragedy suddenly unfolding in his life. And with words that drip with the wisdom granted to those who suffer, he responds in the form of a rhetorical question "Shall we accept good from God, and not trouble?"[4] Job has it right, and so does Naomi. They both understand that their God is big, and He is behind the rescues and the deliverances, the babies born to them as well as the healthy crops. But he is also behind the moments of sheer pain and agony, the days of drought and famine, and the moments of destruction that take your breath away. All are from His hand, which makes them all a gift.

THE GIFT OF PAIN

No way! There is not a chance I want to see pain as a gift. Why would I? Who wants to open that gift anyway? I will tell you who. You do, and so do I.

When did we stop viewing pain as a gift from God? When did we stop thanking Him for the bad as well as the good? We are generally grateful for the gifts we define as "good" that we know come directly from God's hand. I am pretty certain we all have taken some time to thank Him for the blessings we view as outside of our ability to create.

For example, we thank God for allowing us to experience our children, our health, good marriages, even our ability to hold a job and provide for our families. We probably also thank Him for the other kinds of things, such as our mind's ability to know Him and think His thoughts, and our heart's ability to feel and deeply give and receive love. Those are all gifts from God that we like, acknowledge, and thank Him for. We drag them over into His presence and open them up with a flourish. We excitedly pull at the ribbon and tear into the paper, anxious to experience all of what those kinds of gifts can mean in our lives.

But when was the last time we looked at those gifts that are still unopened and not explored? Equally from God's hand, equally generous are those gifts of pain and suffering, those gifts of loneliness, disease, and disability. When was the last time we dragged one of those gifts over into the presence of our God and opened it in front of Him to see what the inside of those dreaded boxes contained?

Pain is one of God's best and most effective instructors. We would rather He chose some other tool to use in our lives, but think for a moment how very effective the use of pain is in giving us direction and focus. Without question, God knows what it takes to recapture our hearts. He loves us enough to not only want our hearts, but to willingly allow them to break and hurt in order that they want Him completely. So what does it look like to open those gifts of pain in front of God? It looks a lot like worship.

For about the next thirty chapters in Job's book we hear him as he opens the gift of suffering. He is loud, a lot like Naomi. God is the subject, God is the One his words are directed at. The book of Job, just like Naomi's great complaint, is all about God, which makes it not only deep, but full of insight and worship.

Job is not an easy book to read at any point in your life, but when you are in the middle of opening one of those gifts of pain and really truly want to know how to receive it, a book like Job really ministers to your heart. It is honest. It is truthful. It is the natural human way to respond to pain. To say "ouch" in about 350 different ways, all in a safe place, all uttered before a God who loves you.

Like Naomi, Job's audience was not only God, but a few close friends who came to cheer him up, famously failing in that endeavor. In an effort to take the high road and defend God and blame Job, they miss the point. As you listen to these men, you can easily imagine all the gifts of pain they have that are unopened in their front room. They simply won't accept pain from the hand of God. Their theology is flawed, and their view of God is hopelessly small.

In the end God comes to Job in awesome, overwhelming power, the kind of power that makes Job exclaim "I thought I knew you but now I have seen you."[5] His eyes see beyond what life holds. In the end of the drama, God comes down and gets in the faces of those three supposed friends and tells them they have been wrong, and they need Job to pray for them, because "everything he said was right."[6]

Think about that for a second, and then go read the fresh, probably unopened pages of the book of Job in your copy of the Bible. As you read that most ancient story, listen to the words Job says about God, words spoken against the backdrop of God's own pronouncements. These words are not only normal, but in God's opinion, correct. Job's words were true and honest, and speaking them brought his heart freedom. Freedom to feel, freedom to express those feelings, and most of all, freedom to call it all worship!

A REQUIRED SACRIFICE

It was a Thursday night toward the end of March in 2008, just a month after Logan's talk to his classmates. In the interim, my boys and I had moved in with my parents as we waited for the house we would rent from a friend to become available. We had not been able to visit Cam as he was acclimating to his new surroundings. As I looked forward to seeing him for the first time, I did so with a great deal of fear and trepidation. I was as anxious to see him as I was nervous at how it would go and how he would respond.

We had never gone to "visit" Cam anywhere; we had only "picked him up." For all those years we never went to "see" him, even at school. Once we walked in the schoolroom door, he was on his way to pick up his backpack, with bright eyes and the word "fries" coming out of his questioning mouth. But as the day finally came for me to go see him at Rainbow House, I knew that this time there would be no "picking up" or "fries." There was only the reality that I was visiting my son at his new home. I had decided to go alone the first time, not knowing what the visit would be like and not wanting to expose my other boys to more pain. Such moments from the past have left incredible images in our minds and hearts.

I arrived that night with dinner for the residents of the house—fried chicken from the grocery store, a healthier choice, barely, than fast food, but still one of Cam's favorites. All the kids were playing outside, so I dropped the groceries in the kitchen and opened the sliding glass door to see Cam sitting alone on a bench in the backyard. He stood up as I approached and immediately said "Fries." I told him "No." As soon as I sat down beside him his shoulders dropped and he began to cry, not in anger, but in a hopeless, defeated kind of knowing way. I will never know the series of thoughts my son had or what kinds of feelings those thoughts brought out of his heart. But what was clear as I sat beside him that day was that I was not there to rescue him and take him home. I was there to visit him.

He sat in silence until it was time for dinner. He and the two other autistic young men also ate in silence. It was very evident as Cam moved from task to task with simple promptings that tremendous growth and learning had taken place in him as he adjusted to his new surroundings. I could clearly see that physically he was responding well to the healthier diet and daily walks the house took. There was a growing sureness I could see in him because of his ability to do the simple tasks expected of him now. But to be totally honest, none of those clear indicators of Cam being in the right place reached my heart. He was still my little boy, and he was not home, and in those painful first moments, his disappointment in me for not taking him there was very clear.

We moved through the evening together, doing his normal activities, watching part of one of his favorite movies. I helped him through his evening shower and brushing his teeth, and then I put him to bed. I knelt beside his very cool boat that now sat in a new room brightly painted in a soft yellow. I looked around at all Cam's pictures of the ocean from home, at his shelves decorated just like they had been in his room at home. It was all the same, yet it could not have been more different.

I stroked Cam's nicely cut hair; a successful trip to the barber had been one of the many new things to celebrate in his first month at Rainbow. But as I played with the brown curls of my son, who looked more like a man than he ever had, I was not thinking about success; I was thinking about loss. I was not opening a gift that I wanted to tear into; I was painfully opening the ribbon and gingerly pulling the tape off of a package I never dreamed God would hand me.

I prayed for my son that night as I had for nearly every night of his thirteen years and ten months. I thanked God for the day, for the provision of this place, and for how well Cam was doing. Then I said, "Amen," and my heart froze. The words that had followed that "amen" for all those many nights were now stuck in my throat like a dry, dense ball. They wanted to come out, they nearly forced their way out, but they were no longer true, no longer applicable. "I will see you in the morning" was swallowed back into my throat like a bitter pill. I put my head on Cam's bed as I stayed there on my knees for many minutes.

Do you know what those moments felt like? They felt like worship. As I knelt, the passage God brought to my mind was very fresh; in fact, it was the one I was preparing to teach the coming week—the story of how Abraham by faith offered his son Isaac as a sacrifice.[7] In that amazing story God did not ultimately require Isaac as a sacrifice; in fact, at the last second He stopped Abraham and instead brought a ram stuck in a thicket to offer up in the place of his son.

It was so clear. I told God, "Wow, this is what it feels like on the other side of the sacrifice, when the ram is not in the thicket, and you require what is being offered." And let me tell you, this separation from Cameron sure felt like a sacrifice! By nature, a sacrifice must cost you something, and without question this one was costly. True worship does cost something. But there is something so sweet about sitting in that place and being willing, to know that act was pleasing to God, not because He is a mean God who requires awful things, but because it was right. It was the right thing at the right time. I will never know what that obedience saved me or my boys from, or for that matter, even saved Cameron from. I just know I was willing, though barely, to offer it. Without question, I have never had to bend my will farther.

A GROVE OF TREES

In my neighborhood, I routinely drive by a small grove of palm trees in the process of being bent to form a unique archway. The trees have been planted several feet apart, and four to five feet up each tree a brace is placed to push it away from its neighbor at the desired angle. All together, the trees are creating an entry in front of a large house, and as I drive by several times a week, I watch the once healthy palm trees submit to the brace. They have gone through a series of stages from green and healthy to withered and yellow, then to dry and brown, with the end product looking almost dead.

Now, however, green is beginning to show through at the tops and is working its way downward. Life has come back to that unique grove, and in the coming months and years I am certain that the healthy trees growing at their unusual angles will become an interesting and enriching part of that stretch of road. But as many people drive by and notice the trees, they will have no idea of the struggle they endured to be formed that way. The braces will be long gone; the dry parts will be replaced by rich, strong, green stalks. There will be no hint of a painful process, only a beautiful result.

That is the way I see those moments in our lives when bending our will is required. It is painful beyond words. The process alone feels for much of the time like it will destroy us, but somehow, as we relinquish our control and submit to the braces put against us, we find that God is doing a new thing and our spark for life is growing back, albeit in a new direction. The difference is remarkable to the onlooker. Many will never know the cost of living life at certain angles, but they appreciate the outcome.

People who live that way are magnetic; others simply want to know them. They have no idea what is involved, but they would give anything just to be like them. That is the great and eternal outcome of a sacrifice or a recaptured heart, because it gives God greater glory. It is a true form of worship. Does it hurt? Absolutely. Do you want to push back against the braces? Yes, all the time, but the truth is that even that effort makes our strength greater as we move in the direction God has called us.

What is God asking you to offer today? What places has He asked for only to hear you say, "No way, you cannot have this." What does that brace feel like, look like, and sound like for you? What would it take to bend your will to His, no matter how hard that is? You know what it is that He is asking for; I bet you already have it in your mind. It might make no sense at all, but you know His voice when you hear it, you know the brace when you feel it. Will you submit to it, will you offer it? Will you give Him the worship He is worthy of?

PURE WORSHIP

One of the many things I have learned from my son Cameron is about worship. Much of Cam's life was spent in our backyard on a patch of grass about ten by fifteen feet. He ran back and forth on that patch until he created a well-worn path. Each day as he ran or skipped along that piece of our backyard, he periodically stopped and looked at something that caught his eye. It might have been as simple as the sun cutting through the trees above him or as complex as a flying insect. Regardless of what caught his attention, one of the things I always enjoyed about those moments with Cam was stopping with him and looking at what he saw in the world. Cam has long possessed a unique world view that is as simple and basic as nature itself. He does not feel at all comfortable interacting with people, but when he finds a safe place where he can experience life silently, he seems to understand it in a way I never will.

As I spent hour after hour with Cam for many years, watching him live in a world very different from mine, I have often contemplated the way in which he will worship God when he someday gets to see Him face to face. I love thinking about sharing heaven with my son in a way that is so deep and is understood by both of us. There are so few places at which we have really been able to connect deeply here, but I long for that interaction with my son and look forward to what it will be like.

However, each time I think about that first conversation, I enjoy even more knowing I will have to wait in line. I know Cam will want to speak with someone else first; he will want to talk to his Creator. He will want to worship. And as I imagine that moment, I think my son will be able to worship God in a way that is so pure that I will never come close to understanding it. He will worship God for what he experienced here, but what we have missed: the beauty of the earth and the complexity of God's creation that so ministered to his heart.

He will not thank Him for the mental and social abilities needed to succeed here, as his brothers will. He will not be able to thank Him for a mind that was completely able to think and communicate the rich thoughts and depths of God that others have known. No, Cam's worship will be so pure because he will give it to his Creator simply because in and of Himself, God is worthy of worship. All of it—His attributes and His power, His holiness and His love—is worthy of our worship, regardless of how those attributes touched our lives. Cam may not know God in the fullness that you and I do now, but I believe the worship he will offer in heaven will be that much greater. The gift of his life or any other life is to reflect God's glory and worship Him. Cam does that and will continue to do that throughout eternity.

One of the many special gifts that come with raising Cam has been learning to understand this very pure form of worship and beginning to express it to God now. Not just thanking Him for what He has done or for the blessings He has provided, but truly acknowledging who He is, whether those attributes are benefiting me in a way I understand or not. That kind of worship really changes the way you view God's gifts. You can truly start to not only unwrap the painful ones, but even to embrace them. The gifts are always good; they are always for our best interests and God's glory. Our job is to learn like Job, like my son, to see God in a new way because of them.

Naomi was learning that lesson as well. Even in the midst of her grief, in the midst of her painful thoughts and memories, despite the famines, despite the death of her hopes and dreams, God was the kind of God who could be worshipped. He was recapturing her heart. Maybe the first moment she began to see that was when she raised her tired eyes to the familiar fields of Bethlehem. To the fields that she had imagined her grandchildren running and playing in, just like their fathers had. The same fields that, with their dry and barren crops, had once driven them away from their home.

Those very same fields were now filled with life; a barley harvest was about to be brought in. There was new life in her home. I wonder if she exhaled at the sight. I wonder if it made her cry to think of how

Elimelech would have dreamed of seeing that field those many years ago, to think of all that might have been different if they had endured the famine there. I wonder if she bowed her head to thank God in the depths of her bitter and searing heart for something that felt like good news, something hopeful, something new.

A NEW THING

The first book of the Bible begins with the story of creation.[8] I love thinking about that, reading that story, even finding application to my life from the truth that we serve a Creator God. A God who made the universe out of what did not exist.[9] Do you know that the very end of the Bible tells us the same thing about God's nature? At the close of the book of Revelation, as the new heavens and new earth are being brought in front of John in his vision, God says, "Behold, I am making all things new."[10]

One of my favorite attributes of God is His ability as Creator God to make something out of nothing, to do a new thing. His creative ability is on display each morning and evening as He paints the sky with a new set of colors and patterns each day to raise the sun and set it again. Each morning provides us with a new chance to know His mercy and faithfulness.[11] And to be sure that we know it is all new for us each day, He makes every twenty-four hours unique, beginning with His painting of the sunrise.

Each season also brings something new. Without question, of all the seasons, spring seems to be the clearest display in nature of the new growth God has brought out. But I can see that work happening all the time in front of my house as my flowers grow and flourish, seemingly each day getting stronger, responding not only to water, but also to sunlight. In their simple way, for the short time they grow they clearly reflect their Creator.

Naomi could experience that in abundance as she walked back into town and saw the previously empty fields now full of barley ripe for the harvest. That would tell her tired mind at least two things that would feel hopeful. First, God really had done a new thing and ended the famine, as she had heard back in Moab. Second, she and Ruth would have food, as Ruth would be allowed, as was the custom, to gather what was left over in the fields near their new home. Something new to think about, something, even in a small way, to begin to hope for. I am certain her heart was still hurting as she looked at those fields. I am sure the pain and truth of her recent angry words still hung in the air. But the reality in front of her was speaking louder than her words. God was faithful, He was providing, He was doing a new thing, and she was finally home.

A New Home

As part of our tremendous transition that spring of 2008, Logan, Boone, and I moved into a new home. My triplets had lived in one home their entire lives. The home we had left was rather new, in an area recently developed in our city. It was just a couple miles from the schools they had always attended, from our church, and from all the normal places and people they knew.

The home we moved into was much smaller than the one we left. It was about five or six miles away from where we had lived before. I had secured transfers for them to attend the same schools, but the transition still was a challenging one. We were packing up many years of stuff, downsizing, and moving into rooms that were small in a house that was older and did not have many of the fancy things we were used to. No large swimming pool and basketball court in the backyard, no familiar friends several doors down to hang out with. It was all new for us.

One of the amazing gifts of a new thing as significant as a home is that it can be made into whatever you can think and desire. My sons moved into our former spacious house as infants. Now they were strong young men carrying the furniture into this new house. Not only were they part of moving us in; they were part of fixing it up. By the time their brother got home from college that spring, the entire house had been painted inside and out by my boys, me, and a team of volunteers from our church. My sons had been part of putting new fixtures in the sinks and new lights. They had helped to pick out the new carpet and tile and had painted the old swing set in the back. They had ownership in this new house, and as owners they have taken pride in how it is maintained, on most days picking their backpacks and shoes up off the floor without being asked. They have often commented on the benefits of not having all those stairs and how quickly they can move from their rooms to the table for a meal. We have done slumber parties in each room of the house and have generally enjoyed this new thing God had for us.

What we have learned most of all is that "home" has little to do with the walls that surround you and everything to do with the people who are there. My boys will always have a home with me. They will always be able to get angry there, be silly there. They will always have moments full of joy and fear, they will be hopeful, and they will be anxious, all right at home.

Our new home looks nothing like our old one. It is a new thing. I am sure those ripened fields looked just as foreign to Naomi as driving up this driveway feels to me, but for both of us, it is a place we can call home.

HONESTY

For some reason, the idea of being truly honest with God about how we feel is a hard one for people to accept. In the midst of the "proper" attitude we have tried to create, what has been lost is the honest exchange God desires for the things He allows in our lives. He has long gone unthanked for many of the gifts He has given us. We endure the suffering and challenges of those gifts of pain, but we miss the reward at the end.

As a result of the view Job got as he looked on his Creator, as he saw the power and majesty and worthiness of the One who allowed the pain in his life, he could not help but worship. He could not be anything but thankful for what his eyes had seen. The same thought must have come over Naomi as she looked at those full fields: God was providing. In the face of all that loss, she was still expectant that God would come through for her. And as she saw the outcome of all that had happened, I am sure she told God she did not even know how to trust Him, but truly she had come home because there was no one else she even wanted to trust.

My son Logan and I had a very difficult night together at the end of the summer several years ago. He had just turned thirteen, and I think it was one of those nights that was a little too hot. We also had tried to cram a few too many things into the day. We were tired, and we all had about twenty-five different things on our minds that could erupt at any minute. We were trying not to lose control. But on this particular night, both Logan and I allowed our frustration to overflow like a volcano, and neither of us felt very good about it, especially me.

When we finally reached home after the last of our miserable errands, I called my son into my room. "Logan, I am so sorry for the way I acted. Please forgive me."

"That's okay, Mom," he responded. "I didn't make very good choices tonight."

"You are right about that. But I responded poorly to your choices. I did the very thing I am always telling you and your brothers not to do—to let everything else that is bothering me influence the way I react to something totally unrelated. I love you, son."

After my apology, Logan walked back silently to his room, but I knew his heart was still hurting. Less than five minutes later I heard his voice in the hallway, calling me. I met him halfway between his room and mine, and he looked me right in the eyes. My little boy, who even at thirteen stood eye to eye with me, looked straight through me and clearly told me the truest and sweetest words I have ever heard him say. He said, "Mom, when you act like that it makes me not want to trust you, but you are the only one I can trust."

I think my heart froze as the truth of those words made their way down to it. I was so discouraged and yet so grateful at the same time. I told him again how very sorry I was for hurting him, and especially for hurting that place of trust in his heart. I told him I had earned that place and I wanted it back, that I loved him and was so thankful he had the courage to tell me that.

Within seconds of my saying those words, Logan responded with, "Okay Mom, do you want to go downstairs and watch a movie?"

I said, a little shocked, "Sure, that would be great."

Once downstairs, he put the movie in and asked if I wanted a soda and popcorn. He then brought them to me and sat down beside me. For two hours we just spent time together. For the life of me, I cannot tell you what we watched, but I will never forget the gift of that time beside my son. When I went to bed that night, I thanked God what felt like a million times over for Logan's heart and his willingness to be honest with me and for the healing that honesty brought to me.

But as always, God has more for us to know than what we merely experience. Logan's response was exactly the one God desires from me at those heart-searing moments when I am face-to-face with a gift of pain I simply do not want to open. He wants me to leave the darkness of my room and make the same courageous choice my son made that night. Logan sat in the dark and decided that his relationship with me was more important to him than the pain in his heart, and he came back to fix it. To honestly tell me what I had done to him.

That is what God was challenging me to do, to really bring it on. What does it do to you when you pull the wrapping off that gift and see what is inside? God expects a response, He expects us to run out of our room and pound our fists on His door and cry out for an explanation. He wants to hear those words I heard from Logan that night. "God, when you do this, when you hand me this gift, this diagnosis, this dream that has died, this disability, this future, this????, it makes me not want to trust You, but You are the only One I can trust." And then He wants us to give Him the same chance Logan had as he stood there, clear-eyed and brave, to hear my response, to hear me own his pain. God will do that for us; He does not have to apologize as I did, but He will own it. He will own it all. And the second He does, we will respond just like Logan did. We will want to be with Him, we will want to serve Him. We will feel whole just to be beside Him.

How long has it been for you since you could feel the closeness of God's presence like that? How many gifts of pain are sitting around the front room of your house unopened? Or maybe you are sitting there holding this book, and you can look and see the torn gift wrapping on the ground, and you are living with the reality of what was in that box of pain. As you sit there in the darkness of your room, you have not found it in you to walk down the hallway, pound on His door, and demand an explanation. You have not acknowledged that the gift was from Him, and even though you don't understand it, you desperately want to. In the depths of your heart you want to understand how to find the words to thank Him for that gift. You want a heart that can worship Him even in this place, that can see Him as worthy, even through the pain. A heart that believes to the core that what you most want is for Him to be allowed to use even *this* to recapture your heart.

I love the words God spoke to His people through His prophet Zephaniah. They feel right to me now as I sit and type, looking out my screen door to the beautiful yard at my new house. They are the right words for Naomi as she enters her hometown with the scent of ripe fields hanging in the air. They are the words that are true for Job as he lived out the greater blessings of the later part of his life. "At that time I will gather you; at that time I will bring you home."[12]

Are they true for you as well? Will you let Him bring you home?

Chapter Six

Contentment

Now Naomi had a relative on her husband's side, from the clan of Elimelech, a man of standing, whose name was Boaz. And Ruth the Moabitess said to Naomi, "Let me go to the fields and pick up the leftover grain behind anyone in whose eyes I find favor."

Naomi said to her, "Go ahead, my daughter."

So she went out and began to glean in the fields behind the harvesters. As it turned out, she found herself working in a field belonging to Boaz, who was from the clan of Elimelech.

Just then Boaz arrived from Bethlehem and greeted the harvesters, "The Lord be with you!"

"The Lord bless you!" they called back.

Boaz asked the foreman of his harvesters, "Whose young woman is that?"

The foreman replied, "She is the Moabitess who came back from Moab with Naomi. She said, 'Please let me glean and gather among the sheaves behind the harvesters.' She went into the field and has worked steadily from morning till now, except for a short rest in the shelter."

So Boaz said to Ruth, "My daughter, listen to me. Don't go and glean in another field and don't go away from here. Stay here with my servant girls. Watch the field where the men are harvesting, and follow along after the girls. I have told the men not to touch you. And whenever you are thirsty, go and get a drink from the water jars the men have filled."

At this, she bowed down with her face to the ground. She exclaimed, "Why have I found such favor in your eyes that you notice me—a foreigner?"

Boaz replied, "I've been told all about what you have done for your mother-in-law since the death of your husband—how you left your father and mother and your homeland and came to live with a people you did not know before. May the Lord repay you for what you have done. May you be richly rewarded by the Lord, the God of Israel, under whose wings you have come to take refuge."

"May I continue to find favor in your eyes, my lord," she said. "You have given me comfort and have spoken kindly to your servant— though I do not have the standing of one of your servant girls."

At mealtime Boaz said to her, "Come over here. Have some bread and dip it in the wine vinegar." When she sat down with the harvesters, he offered her some roasted grain. She ate all she wanted and had some left over. As she got up to glean, Boaz gave orders to his men, "Even if she gathers among the sheaves, don't embarrass her. Rather, pull out some stalks for her from the bundles and leave them for her to pick up, and don't rebuke her."

So Ruth gleaned in the field until evening. Then she threshed the barley she had gathered, and it amounted to about an ephah. She carried it back to town, and her mother-in-law saw how much she had gathered. Ruth also brought out and gave her what she had left over after she had eaten enough. Her mother-in-law asked her, "Where did you glean today? Where did you work? Blessed be the man who took notice of you!"

Then Ruth told her mother-in-law about the one at whose place she had been working. "The name of the man I worked with today is Boaz," she said.

"The Lord bless him!" Naomi said to her daughter-in-law. "He has not stopped showing his kindness to the living and the

dead." She added, "That man is our close relative; he is one of our kinsman-redeemers."

Then Ruth the Moabitess said, "He even said to me, 'Stay with my workers until they finish harvesting all my grain.'"

Naomi said to Ruth her daughter-in-law, "It will be good for you, my daughter, to go with his girls, because in someone else's field you might be harmed." So Ruth stayed close to the servant girls of Boaz to glean until the barley and wheat harvests were finished. And she lived with her mother-in-law.[1]

THE BACKPACK

IT WAS A rainy morning sometime last winter. I was driving my sons Logan and Boone to their junior high school. We were on time, within the window of ten to fifteen minutes before school begins. As on all rainy days, my fellow Southern California drivers and I were struggling with the elements, causing some backup in traffic. But as I pulled up to the school and turned to the backseat to tell my boys good-bye, Boone's face looked ashen and grim. He slowly informed me why. "I forgot my backpack, Mom" was his simple yet emotion-packed sentence.

As soon as the words were spoken there was this energetic yet silent interchange between my thirteen-year-old Boone and me. My thoughts went something like, *I could run home and get the backpack and drop it off at the front office before my first meeting.*

And as I looked at the pleading blue eyes of my son, I knew that behind those eyes his thoughts were saying something similar: *Mom could run home and grab my backpack before she goes to the office; it would take only fifteen minutes.*

I broke the silence with a statement that frankly shocked us both. I said, "Boone, you will have to go to school without it today." His face turned another shade of pale, while Logan took off toward the campus, not wanting to be in the middle of this one.

When Boone told me he could not go to school without his backpack, I asked, "Is there something in it that has to be turned in today?"

He said "No, but I will be in trouble from every teacher."

I shook my head and told him I was sorry for the kind of day he would have, but this time I would not go home to get it. Boone took his seat belt off and got out of the car in silence. He was not angry; he was more shocked, and I am certain he was a bit disappointed in me for not coming through for him.

I drove off, turned the corner, and headed the several miles to our church to start my workday. As I was driving, I called a close friend of mine. She and I had spoken on the phone the night before about some of the struggles she was having setting boundaries for her adult son. I told her that in a very small way I could understand how hard that was, and I relayed the story about the backpack. My friend responded with incredible truth. "Becky, do you know why that was so hard? Because you could have fixed it, and you chose not to." Wow, was that ever a concise statement about how it feels in your heart as a parent when you hold the line with your kids.

As I hung up the phone and continued on my short drive to work, it did not take long before I thought of a much deeper meaning of that little story for me. My thoughts started with my concern about how Boone must be feeling. I tried to put myself in his shoes, and I quickly caught my breath. I have been in his shoes many times. In fact, several times that very week I had gone to God needing a "backpack" of some kind. I had the same pale, shocked look on my face as the reality of how the consequences of one of my poor choices or the choice of someone else, or even the outcome of God's choice, was going to feel. I distinctly remember asking God to fix it. The same thoughts went through my mind that had passed through my son's. *God could fix it; it would only take him fifteen seconds or so. My goodness, He could snap his fingers and make this go away.*

But the truth that made me drive away from my son's school in the direction of my office rather than home is the same one God uses when He withholds the backpacks we desperately plead for. My desire to do what is best for my son pales in comparison to not only God's desire, but to His perfect ability to always *do* what is best for me. The kicker is that I know full well that God could fix it, and He is choosing not to. On many days this leaves me standing by the side on the curb like my son, with a look of shock and disappointment.

The thing I pulled away from that entire scenario is that God always gives us what we need, not necessarily what we want. That gets problematic when you don't really want what you actually need, but are convinced that you badly need what you want.

What my son learned that day in a way he did not greatly appreciate is that though he wanted his backpack very much, he apparently did not need it. He actually made it through the day in an uneventful kind of way. And, may I add, he has never forgotten his backpack since! In the same way, the several backpacks I asked God for during the last week, although maybe legitimate, were not needed by me, or God would have provided them. His withholding of anything we ask for is only for our best interest. I know Boone learned more from my not fixing his mistake than he would have had I gone home to retrieve his backpack.

I, too, learn from doing without some of my wants, just as Boone did. So what do you do when you don't get the backpack you asked for? Maybe we can all learn from Ruth about how to want what you need. And just maybe when we learn to do that, we will find a whole new definition of being content.

WANTING WHAT YOU NEED

Once they got settled, Ruth wasted no time addressing their greatest need. She set out to find food for Naomi and herself. I am sure Ruth had long ago forgotten how to even identify a want in her mind and heart, let alone a dream for something beyond mere survival. No, Ruth knew only needs, and strong, basic ones at that. But there is hope on the horizon. As we watch Ruth begin to take hold of that hope, she does so in the most correct way. She does not try to define that hope, and she does not demand its fulfillment. She is busy, she is purposeful, and most of all, she is content, because all she wants is what she actually needs. She just does the next thing that is necessary; she sets out to find food. In her simple act we can learn so much, because in our civilized society we truly need little and want a lot!

The requests for God to fix things, to grab our backpacks, comes from every direction. In His immense love and patience He continues to grant only what is needed. I believe He would point us gently to this little chapter of the Bible to see a woman who does it right. Ruth reminds us that wanting what you need leads to blessings you can never imagine. It truly allows us to begin to hope in a way that cannot be defined and, more importantly, cannot be defeated. And that kind of hope leads us to contentment.

THE RIGHT FIELD

As the next chapter in the book of Ruth opens, we find ourselves quickly moving from a tragedy to the makings of a very cool love story. Ruth begins by addressing the need for daily provisions. In that culture it was a normal practice for women to follow behind the harvesters and get whatever dropped as they gathered in the crops. Knowing this custom, Ruth grabbed a basket and wasted no time finding a field in which to gather for the day. She found the right field, the one owned by a man named Boaz, our handsome hero. Ruth has already been working a good portion of the day by the time he arrives on the scene.

Boaz enters our story greeting his workers warmly. He is a gentleman of some standing in the community, one to whom others look to for input in the middle of a discussion. As we see him interact with those in his employ, he seems to be the kind of boss everyone wanted to see come around. But there is much more to Boaz than the very kind, gracious, generous man we meet as the chapter opens. The encounter we are about to look at was well planned, though not by either party involved. God knew the exact thing Ruth would need on this day, and He brought it to her in the person of Boaz. But in order to know how great a plan it was, you have to go back many years.

THINGS PLANNED LONG AGO

God always has more in mind than we think, believe, or even could imagine. Listen to these very true words spoken by the prophet Isaiah. "O Lord you are my God; I will exalt you and praise your name, for in perfect faithfulness you have done marvelous things, things planned long ago."[2]

The "long ago" in our story was around the time in Israel's history when they were about to enter the Promised Land. Moses had turned over the reigns of the nation of Israel to Joshua. The new leader had boldly led the people across the Jordan River at flood stage, as God miraculously parted the water. After crossing the Jordan, the first big city they came to was Jericho. Joshua sent two spies into the city to scout it out, for it was no ordinary city; even in the violent Near East few cities were built like Jericho. It was literally a fortress, with huge, thick stone walls and a gate that opened for only certain periods of time throughout the day to give access to the city, but closed tightly when it became dark.

The spies spent the day there, and as dusk came, they ducked into a house just before the gates closed. The house they ended up in was inhabited by a woman named Rahab. Not long after the frightened men entered, there came another knock on the door. Someone had seen the spies and had informed the king that they had gone into Rahab's house. She quickly hid the men and answered the door, telling the soldiers standing there that those men had indeed come into her house, but they had left and probably had made it through the gate before it closed. She encouraged them to hurry, since they still might be able to catch the spies.

As soon as the soldiers left her house, Rahab went up on the roof where the Israelite spies had hid to tell them they were safe. Before she lowered them down the city wall from her window, this courageous woman had an amazing talk with them. Listen to her words as she communicates clearly where her hope is placed and how desperately she wants what she needs.

"I know," she began, "that the Lord has given this land to you and that a great fear of you has fallen on us, so that all who live in this country are melting in fear because of you. We have heard how the Lord dried up the water of the Red Sea for you when you came out of Egypt, and what you did to Sihon and Og, the two kings of the Amorites east of the Jordan, whom you completely destroyed. When we heard of it, our hearts melted and everyone's courage failed because of you, for the Lord your God is God in heaven above and on the earth below. Now then, please swear to me by the Lord that you will show kindness to my family, because I have shown kindness to you. Give me a sure sign that you will spare the lives of my father and mother, my brothers and sisters, and all who belong to them, and that you will save us from death."[3]

Those words sound a little familiar. They sound like Ruth's words on the hillside that day overlooking Moab. They sound like they come from a person who would never settle for less, once she heard who God really is and what He wants from her. She, like Ruth, was a foreigner and like Ruth, she desperately wanted more out of life. And again like Ruth, she made a courageous choice to get it. After her passionate plea and the men's agreement to save her, she lowered the men to safety. The instruction they left her with was to hang a red cord out of her window so they could rescue her and her family when Jericho was raided.

The Israelites took the city by the most unconventional means, as they marched around it and yelled, bringing the thick stone walls down. Rahab and her family were welcomed into the camp of the Israelites. And the courageous and faithful Rahab caught the eye of a young man named Salmon of the Ephraimites, a large and influential tribe in Israel. Together they had a son and named him Boaz—the same Boaz we see walk into Ruth's life in just the right way at just the right time, with just the right kind of appreciation for a foreign woman who desired to know God enough to make a bold and courageous choice. His entire life he had grown up hearing the stories of what his mother had done in rescuing the spies. Now in his very field worked a woman with the same desire to know this powerful God, a woman with tremendous need, a woman who that very day, without her knowledge, was about to meet her redeemer. Ruth was about to come face-to-face with the one who would satisfy her needs in a way far surpassing what she could want or even hope for.

THE MEETING

As Boaz greeted his men, he must have caught sight of Ruth out of the corner of his eye. She was a very beautiful woman. She would have looked different from all the other women, as she would still be wearing clothes and jewelry according to the customs of Moab. Boaz asked his foreman about her and was given a very good report. The foreman told him about Ruth's choice to leave Moab and care for Naomi after her own husband had died. He also told Boaz about how hard Ruth had been working in the field all that day.

Boaz then turns to Ruth to welcome her to his field. He has already made provisions for her safety and has made sure his men would not harm her in any way. He invites her to help herself to the water and anything else she needs. Ruth is overwhelmed by this act of kindness from the owner of the field and asks him why he would be so kind to a foreigner like her. Boaz's response is gentle and gracious. He affirms her for her selfless care of Naomi and for leaving all she knew to come and live in Bethlehem. He finishes his answer to Ruth with one of the most beautiful blessings in the Bible: "May the Lord repay you for what you have done. May you be richly rewarded by the Lord, the God of Israel, under whose wings you have come to take refuge."[4]

Talk about recapturing your heart! Any woman's heart would basically melt to hear those words from a man! I love their first meeting. Boaz commends her and at the same time focuses her attention on the One who has the ultimate blessing for her, the One who will truly give her what she needs. But Boaz also shows himself more than willing to help her adjust to her new life. He invites her to sit with him at the afternoon meal and instructs his men to be sure to drop a lot of extra stalks of grain so that she will be able to take home enough food for both herself and Naomi.

In their first meeting, Boaz protected her as well as provided for her needs in the most sensitive way. After all the struggles we have walked through with Ruth, doesn't it just make you smile to see her treated so very kindly?

She brings her armfuls of barley back to Naomi, and her mother-in-law is overwhelmed with the amount. Her astonishment turns to joy when she hears at whose field Ruth has been working. Ruth was at the right field for more than one reason. As it turns out, Boaz was a near relative of Elimelech, Naomi's husband. In that culture, Boaz was in a unique position to help Naomi and Ruth. I am sure that for the first time in years Ruth saw what looked like a smile appear on the wrinkled face of Naomi. For the first time in a very long time Naomi had hope. It was certainly faith that had brought both her and Ruth on the long journey home. Looking at the pile of barley on the table would ignite that faith as hope, hope that would eventually bring about something Naomi probably had not known for the many years since she left that spot: contentment.

Each day Ruth was in action. She was obedient. She was meeting their needs. All she wanted in the coming days was to go to the same field every morning and gather the provisions she and Naomi would need for the day. She followed behind the harvesters in the field of Boaz each day of the harvest. Never once did she move out of line and gather grain ahead of them; she simply picked up what they dropped for her. And each evening she came home content, because God had given them what they needed for the day. Little did she know all that God was doing or had done in the heart of the man in whose field she was working. Ruth just kept doing the same thing. She didn't know that each morning as she went to work she was gathering at the feet of her redeemer.

WHAT TO HOPE FOR?

I don't know about you, but the surest way for me to feel immediately discontent is to hope for something to change! I get to a place in my life where I know basically what to expect. For the most part I remember my backpack, I have most of what I need, and I don't demand much more than that. I feel like I am pretty content in that place. But if I am not careful, what I am doing is living a life that requires no faith, thus eliminating a place for God to work and do some amazing things. I can be so busy living my life that I forget to ask Him for the abundant life He promised me.

My life is routinely overwhelming. I think when life is like that all the time, you really get to the point at which you give God one of those sideways glances when you read about how "hope is an anchor for your soul"[5] and then say "God, come on, do you expect me to do all this and still hope You will give me more?" That act of hope does not even seem possible, but that is exactly what He expects. As you open that Pandora's box called hope, however, you must do so with the understanding that your hope must be defined only by God. Because as we begin to hope, we start needing what we want very quickly, and contentment goes out the window. And we are sitting in the backseat of a car, pleading for a backpack.

Living Without the Backpack

I don't know what backpack you might be asking for. I don't know what place in your life and heart is stirring for more than you have experienced. Maybe you long for a new job or career. Maybe you yearn for the child you have always wanted. Possibly you have asked for your health to be restored, or for energy to live your life the way you used to. Maybe you would love to have a home and financial stability. You could do without the backpack, but for some reason, right at this moment you don't really feel like getting out of the car, like Boone had to. You basically are waiting for God to come through. After all, He is God. He could do it. *It would not even be a hard thing for Him,* you think as you sit there waiting, putting your life on hold as you spend each day dreaming and hoping, sure that you need what you want.

I have done that. I have probably asked for several different kinds of things in the past. One thing I know I have allowed my heart to begin to hope for has been in the area of a relationship. I have been very willing to sit there all day with God, asking for a relationship backpack in the form of a great guy!

I am a single mom of four growing teenage boys. I have been single for quite a while now. Many holidays have passed where I attended the staff Christmas party alone, feeling a bit awkward and out of place. I have walked into hundreds of church services where I quickly moved to the side of the auditorium to sit by myself. Many times I don't even notice it, but when I am in the middle of hoping for more I am no longer content to sit alone. In fact, as I walk into that huge auditorium I feel about eight feet tall. I feel like everyone must notice that I am standing there alone, feeling so obviously awkward. As I find my seat, I am relieved just to be out of reach of everyone's stares.

I know many people in our church because I work there. They are all my friends and would never think anything but welcoming thoughts toward me. They would gladly make room for me. But the truth is, I don't want them to scoot over; I want to have someone there with a seat just for me. I don't want to have to scan the crowd for an inconspicuous spot; I want a place that is saved, someone waving for me to come over. So on several different occasions I have found myself in the backseat of a car, demanding a backpack, telling God in no uncertain terms that I need what I want. I am in a famine, and I am done with it. I am not about to go looking for a man in Moab, but I sure want Him to bring me one.

During that time, I have experienced several different relationships. I have learned much from each of the short times I have chosen to actually spend time with a man. But those times were brief in comparison to the amount of time I have spent dreaming about them. Most of my energy and time have been directed toward the dream rather than toward the reality of actually experiencing a relationship.

Ultimately God brought me several backpacks in the form of very nice, godly men. But as I looked at those brief relationships closely, it did not take me very long to realize that, as much as I really wanted a relationship, as much as I dreamed of what it would be like, once I actually experienced parts of it, I did not need it in the form I was pursuing. Instead, those men have become friends that God has used to encourage me and enrich my life.

I realize that aspects of going without this backpack are challenging, I chose to do it. I see the overwhelming benefits of living single, given the unique needs and blessings my life holds in terms of my children, my call to ministry, and my deeper dreams and desires. When I looked at these needs and benefits, the decision was not even close.

The realization of that was as clear as it was heartbreaking. A relationship was not what I needed. Hope has an interesting way of blurring the line between reality and dreams. Walking away from a backpack like that, saying goodbye to a very clearly defined dream and hope leaves you more than a little shell-shocked.

When I finally said "no" to the backpack of a relationship, I was thinking very clearly. I was not being rash. I had prayed through it all, and I had plenty of counsel.

There was one problem, though. Significant corners of my heart flat out boycotted the decision to live without a relationship. In fact, those parts of my heart were so forceful that they kept me up for days, watching old romance movies and eating ice cream on my couch. Gone was the disciplined lifestyle of running, eating healthy, and getting rest, all of which had previously allowed me to lose a ton of weight and fit in my "skinny" jeans. In its place now was the frustrated little girl who did not get what she wanted and was making lots of noise, eating everything in the fridge, and being, quite honestly, a little annoying!

The truth is that as much as I appear tremendously confident, strong and self-assured, I am not. And as much as I have always assumed the role of "one of the guys," I am not, nor do I like to be treated like one! What I really have liked all along, and more recently, too, was acting like a girl, spending an hour I did not have getting ready in front of the mirror, and dreaming about a boy who would come and sweep me off my feet. This was a pattern.

I think that when you are single, especially after being married for so long, you tend to be very hard on yourself. The natural things a partner would do for you to help you slow down and enjoy life are now gone. Life without such a partner is more challenging; now you yourself have to make things happen. This way of living is, in a sense, more serious, but it does not have to be without fun and without advantages all its own. I have learned over time to figure out what I really like in new, refreshing ways I never thought about before, from the way I choose to decorate my house to the things I do when I have time to myself. The advantages of living this new life have never been more clear than when I have said "no" to the backpack of a relationship.

When I have looked at all I wanted in a man and then said that, in my situation, I did not need that type of relationship, I was startled. But that decision also continues to be very good for me, because I am making the choice; it is not something I am doing out of default. I am choosing to want what I need.

Don't get me wrong. I love marriage, I love guys; that is my problem. That is why I morph into a junior higher at the thought of one! I have seen God bless many second marriages and use them for His glory. I have many friends who have been given the amazing gift from God of a great guy, one who will love them and their family. It is possible. But it is also possible that being single is the gift God has for you.

I have never felt comfortable when single women tell me point blank that God is their husband. However, I do believe there is a unique calling and opportunity to serve God without distraction when you are single. I have seen its clear benefits. But I have learned that it is also a lifestyle that needs to be done with a good, healthy dose of sensitivity to my own needs.

God is my husband, but He is not sleeping in bed with me. He is not there to fix my faucet and He does not have a voice when I need to stand strong and hold the line with one of my sons. No, that is done by me. God is my husband, He is that strong presence in my life, but He chooses to use my voice to demand the things I need. He has used me to say "no" to people and things that would not be healthy for me. He has enabled me to make decisions that are best for myself and for my sons. He has empowered me to make impossible choices on behalf of my family regarding my son Cameron, because it was the right thing for our safety and for his future. God has strengthened me to make all those decisions I longed for a man to make on my behalf. Is that romantic? No. Is it good? Yes.

As I gradually learn how to listen to the parts of me that have not had their needs met perfectly in the past, I believe God will allow me to continue to grow and flourish as a single woman. I even went into one of my favorite restaurants the other day and asked for a "table for one," first time ever. I sat there and read a good book the entire time and loved it. Do I still want the backpack? At times, but I am truly enjoying learning to take hold of the freedom that life holds without it.

Once you get out of the backseat of the car without the backpack, you can realize there is lots to enjoy about wanting to live the life God knows you need to live. It seemed that once the boundary line was clear, I could really begin to enjoy what God had for me inside of it.

BOUNDARIES

Before we move on to how to take hold of God's blessings, I want to spend just a couple more minutes on how to turn away from those backpacks we have demanded for what seems like a lifetime. I am not about to tell you that the transition to such a life is easy, but it can be good. It can be very exciting to see what God has for us when we no longer demand the backpack, when we observe a boundary line and turn to see what God has inside it, not beyond it.

Let's look at some of the boundaries God has used in the past. There were twelve tribes in Israel. Ten of them were made up of the sons of Jacob, the grandson of Abraham. The final two tribes came from Jacob's grandsons, Ephraim and Manasseh, the sons of his beloved son Joseph. Each tribe bore the name of its ancestor. Each ancestor had his story, although some of the stories were more interesting and troublesome than others. Each of the tribes was represented as Joshua finally led the people into the Promised Land and distributed the territory among them. Each parcel of land was divided from its neighbor by a boundary God set.

Interestingly, the boundaries were most often natural parts of the landscape, like mountains, a river, or the sea. This meant that lines that showed where one tribe's land ended and another began were often beautiful. But what happened at times was that a tribe, or in this case two tribes, thought they did not have enough land.

Near the end of the book of Joshua, we are given an amazing lesson in contentment, in wanting what you need and going after that need with abandon.

The tribes represented by Joseph's two sons were unhappy with the allotment of land they had received. They were large tribes, and apparently parts of their territory were still occupied by the Canaanites. So instead of getting at the work in front of them and clearing that area of its foreign occupants, they complained to Joshua about the boundary lines, about the amount of land they had been given. They stood at the edge of one of those lines and told Joshua to move it and give them more territory. They asked for a backpack; they thought they needed what they wanted. From the place that overlooked the beautiful ravine that bordered their territory they shouted their demands for more land to Joshua.

In response, the wise leader turned their argument on end and challenged them to look inside the boundaries for God's richest blessing. "But Joshua said to the house of Joseph—to Ephraim and Manasseh—'You are numerous and very powerful. You will have not only one allotment but the forested hill country as well. Clear it, and its farthest limits will be yours; though the Canaanites have iron chariots and though they are strong, you can drive them out.'"[6]

As Joshua walked away, he must have done so with the weary but satisfied smile of a parent who has just held the line with a strong-willed child, and in doing so has given that child a chance to really see what she or he is made of. To find out what is inside the boundaries is a great thing. But often it is not the natural thing for us to do. I don't know about you, but I have found myself there, alongside a boundary, shouting over the ravine to God, telling Him in no uncertain terms about what I wanted. In response, what I was given was an opportunity to turn around and find out what life inside the boundaries looks like and to enjoy the freedom and sense of accomplishment of really clearing things out and finding what life inside the farthest limits looks like.

When was the last time you turned from a firm boundary line and looked at the land inside it? It can be pretty exciting to see what the unexplored parts of our lives look like. What those forested regions contain are God's blessings—simple, clear, new, exciting. It is what Ruth found that day in the field of Boaz—an invitation to know God's blessing.

BLESSINGS

Boaz's words are pretty remarkable, are they not? Listen to them again: "May the Lord repay you for what you have done. May you be richly rewarded by the Lord, the God of Israel, under whose wings you have come to take refuge."[7]

What Boaz was referring to in the "what you have done" portion of that passage is Ruth's choice back on the hillside overlooking Moab. When she decided to not walk down that hill with Orpah, when she said "no" to what she probably wanted in favor of what she needed—it was that for which she would be richly rewarded.

Now Ruth's reward is obvious. Beyond that very cool ending to this neat little book, we are told she is the grandmother of King David, which puts her almost smack dab in the center of the line of Christ. And if that was not enough, God felt she was important enough not only to be mentioned in the Bible, but to have an entire book named after her. I would say those are "rich" rewards! As she looked down the path toward Bethlehem, in her wildest dreams and hopes she never would have conjured up images of those kinds of realities. When she turned her back on the familiar hills and cities of Moab to walk beside Naomi toward the God of Israel, she could have not believed all that awaited her there.

But that is what happens when you are simply obedient. Your wants become your needs and you live a life of contentment. You spend less time in the backseat of the car demanding the backpack and more time enjoying the light and easy way life feels without it on your back. You go after the life God created you to live; you hope, you dream, and all of a sudden, all of those previous images are surpassed, because the truth is that you could never dream that big.

PROMISES

For me, the blessings of God are the workings of His promises in our lives. They can take many forms. But most of all, they are what we experience here as we live our lives on earth, moving toward an eternity that is truly beyond all the blessings we have ever known.

I view God's promises as more eternal than His blessings. We can know some of them here, but for many of His promises, simply hope in them is all we truly need to live contented lives, even if those lives do not hold many of His obvious, tangible blessings. The tool required for that kind of contentment is faith.

Hebrews 11 has long been called the Heroes of Faith chapter. In it you find stories of men and women who demonstrated faith as they lived their lives—lives that for some held tremendous challenges and required strong and sacrificial acts of courage and obedience.

We have talked about some of the guys mentioned there before, but we have not yet mentioned Moses, one of the persons who figures prominently in that Hebrews chapter. "By faith Moses, when he had grown up, refused to be known as the son of Pharaoh's daughter. He chose to be mistreated along with the people of God rather than to enjoy the pleasures of sin for a short time. He regarded disgrace for the sake of Christ as of greater value than the treasures of Egypt, because he was looking ahead to his reward. By faith he left Egypt, not fearing the king's anger; he persevered because he saw him who is invisible."[8]

I love that: he persevered because he saw the God who is invisible. What a true description of faith. And in that short set of verses we are given an accurate description of what a life of faith might contain. He chose mistreatment rather than pleasure of sin, disgrace rather than the treasures of Egypt. In return, Moses got fearlessness, perseverance, and rewards. The fearlessness was developed in the midst of severe struggle, the perseverance came in the face of amazing obstacles, and the rewards came, for the most part, in heaven.

Moses would spend the better part of his life leading a million or so complaining Israelites through a wilderness. As an entire generation of disobedient people died out, God raised up a new generation and a new leader to take them into the Promised Land. At the end of his life the only part of the promise that Moses received was a glimpse of that land seen from a mountaintop. The Promise for him was not tied up in the land; the Promise was in God Himself. He learned to want what he needed, to be content dying just that much short of actually experiencing the Promised Land.

Moses was not the only one who learned contentment from his faith. Listen to a broader description from the book of Hebrews: "All these people were still living by faith when they died. They did not receive the things promised; they only saw them and welcomed them from a distance. And they admitted that they were aliens and strangers on earth. People who say such things show that they are looking for a country of their own. If they had been thinking of the country they had left, they would have had opportunity to return. Instead, they were longing for a better country—a heavenly one. Therefore God is not ashamed to be called their God, for he has prepared a city for them."[9]

Can you do that? Can you live life even if you know full well that you may not receive what you hope for? Will you keep moving even if the better part of life comes in eternity rather than here? The amazing thing about such a life of faith is that the more you live it, the more you seem to love the way life feels here as you look forward to what is coming. All of a sudden, going to the fields each day to pick up behind the harvesters just to get enough for today is very fulfilling. All of a sudden, walking around without the backpack we asked for seems very freeing. This life is exciting; it is both outside of our control and bigger than our plans. The promise no longer seems rooted in what we can have or experience; rather, the promise is in God Himself. How can anything really beat that?

THE GOOD VERSUS THE BEST

I have one of those newer cell phones, those that can do everything for you. I can get my emails from the office and check my schedule and the weather on it, and it's all at my fingertips. Of course, when I first got it I was unable to even make a call as I tried to find the numbers on the many buttons on my new phone. My sons more or less patiently helped me begin to understand the new technology, telling me I lost all credit for having a "cool" phone when I needed my reading glasses just to find the numbers. But I have plodded through, and as of this writing, I not only can send and receive emails and take calls; I have even sent several text messages!

One of the many new things I had to learn on my phone was how to program the alarm clock. To my great delight, the first morning I was awakened by a pleasantly loud chime. I quickly found the snooze button and gave myself the gift of five more minutes. As the mornings went on, I realized my phone had many options to allow me access to that button. In fact, just about every button allowed me to snooze, while there was only one button that turned off the alarm and required me to stand up and put my feet on the floor to start my day.

That much freedom is dangerous for someone like me, for I definitely am not a morning person. It's easier to just reach over and pound the phone almost indiscriminately than it is to precisely hit that one right button. The best button. All the other buttons will give you something that seems good, in this case five more minutes. But only one button will give you the best thing: a trip out of bed. In a world with so many good options, we need to learn to find the right button. We need to stop hitting the snooze and really wake up to begin living the best life we can, the exact life God created us to live.

Are you doing that? If you are sitting in the backseat of a car asking for a backpack, chances are you have just hit the snooze button again and are pleading for something good in your life, but possibly not for the best thing. The best, the farthest limits hold a life with equal parts of excitement and hope. It's all about wanting what you need. I can't give you a formula, but I will simply tell you that you will know it when you begin to live it, and there is nothing like it. You won't find it if you are looking for things "easy" or "happy" or "pleasurable." You find it when you look for gifts like endurance and perseverance, when you find the farthest limits, when you hit the field each day with basket in hand to find what is there for you—contentment. There is nothing like it. In a world looking for good, it is the best life!

Chapter Seven

Redeemer

———✠———

One day Naomi her mother-in-law said to her, "My daughter, should I not try to find a home for you, where you will be well provided for? Is not Boaz, with whose servant girls you have been, a kinsman of ours? Tonight he will be winnowing barley on the threshing floor. Wash and perfume yourself, and put on your best clothes. Then go down to the threshing floor, but don't let him know you are there until he has finished eating and drinking. When he lies down, note the place where he is lying. Then go and uncover his feet and lie down. He will tell you what to do." "I will do whatever you say," Ruth answered. So she went down to the threshing floor and did everything her mother-in-law told her to do.

When Boaz had finished eating and drinking and was in good spirits, he went over to lie down at the far end of the grain pile. Ruth approached quietly, uncovered his feet and lay down. In the middle of the night something startled the man, and he turned and discovered a woman lying at his feet. "Who are you?" he asked. "I am your servant Ruth," she said. "Spread the corner of your garment over me, since you are a kinsman-redeemer." "The Lord bless you, my daughter," he replied. "This kindness is greater than that which you showed earlier: You have not run after the younger men, whether rich or poor. And now, my daughter, don't be afraid.

I will do for you all you ask. All my fellow townsmen know that you are a woman of noble character. Although it is true that I am near of kin, there is a kinsman-redeemer nearer than I. Stay here for the night, and in the morning if he wants to redeem, good; let him redeem. But if he is not willing, as surely as the Lord lives I will do it. Lie here until morning.

So she lay at his feet until morning, but got up before anyone could be recognized; and he said, "Don't let it be known that a woman came to the threshing floor." He also said, "Bring me the shawl you are wearing and hold it out." When she did so, he poured into it six measures of barley and put it on her. Then he went back to town. When Ruth came to her mother-in-law, Naomi asked, "How did it go, my daughter?" Then she told her everything Boaz had done for her and added, "He gave me these six measures of barley, saying, 'Don't go back to your mother-in-law empty-handed.'" Then Naomi said, "Wait, my daughter, until you find out what happens. For the man will not rest until the matter is settled today."[1]

MY TEENAGE SONS Logan and Boone greatly enjoy video games. Their taste in game choices reflects the clear differences in their unique personalities. I have never chosen to participate in their games, but I have long been an admirer as I watch both their skill and the amazing graphics these devices hold. Suffice it to say, they are a far cry from the games of my youth, where lines and dots filled the screen with excitement. Recently my son Boone saved his allowance for an extended period of time for a specific sports game for his video system. He researched the best prices for the game online, and finally, when he had the required money, I took him to our local video game shop to make his big purchase.

After arriving back at home, Boone burst into the house and started playing the game he had carefully unwrapped during our short drive from the store. Within an hour he came out of his room looking very discouraged. He told me as he grabbed the laptop that the game was impossible and he had no idea how to begin to play it in a way that was fun. So he began a search of the internet for "cheats." I have watched my sons do this before, and each time it fascinates me. What Boone was looking for were the secrets or cheats to beat the game. This concept has taken me a while to get my brain around. Apparently the creators of the game release some hints to websites about how to be more successful in advancing in the game. Is that crazy or what? But no matter, there was Boone, furiously scrawling down the codes that would unlock his new game so he could enjoy it to its fullest.

The outcome of those secret codes allowed Boone to fully engage all the components that made the game so desirable to him in the first place. He never was told the secret of how to win; he was just given the ability to compete.

That crazy concept has played around in my mind, hitting its far corners and bringing out some deeper ideas than those you can maneuver on your video game. What Boone did was simply to ask the creator of the game how to play when he was stuck. He basically said, "How does this work? How can I have fun with what you have made?" If you move with me in your imagination, I believe you will see that simple request my son made is not far off from the one we are allowed to make of God. Our Creator. Our Redeemer.

We can come to Him with a disgruntled kind of look similar to the one on Boone's face, shake our heads and say, "Wait a minute, I am stuck here; how in the world does this work? Do you have any ideas to enable me to enjoy this life you created for me to live?"

Let me tell you, that is the exact kind of question God loves to hear. He is the creator of your life, and He knows all the "cheats," the secret codes that open doors to unknown adventure. It all begins with that question about God's ideas for your life, a question rooted in a strong desire to share this life with the One who created us to live it. As soon as we ask, He is ready to unfold the plan; in fact, His greatest desire is to sit right down and play it out with us. Can you imagine what would happen if you handed Him the controller for a minute and actually asked Him to play along, to get you out of a tough spot, to help you reach the next level?

That is exactly what He wants to do. That is what a Redeemer is. One who knows what you need before you do and is waiting to provide you with all that is necessary for you to move forward. The key, though, is that you must first acknowledge a need. That was not hard for Boone. He was clearly overmatched when he attempted to play the game. Not hard for us either, as we face some of our famines head-on. Not hard for Ruth either. She was in the middle of a very tough place as she approached her redeemer. She needed more than the secrets, more than the cheats to get her through her challenges; she needed someone to take the controls. And she was willing to hand them over to someone who was pleased to live life right beside her.

YOUR REDEEMER

Do you believe that of your Redeemer? Do you believe that God wants to share your life? Do you think in your wildest dreams that He not only wants to share with you the secrets of how to make this life work, but that He also wants to get down there and live it with you? Do you think He cares about all the integral parts of your life that make it so interesting to live? He sure does. Just like the creator of Boone's game, He does not want you to miss a single part of what could make it so fun to live. He created this life for you. Who else would you go to for ideas about how to enjoy every part of it to the fullest? Every part. Even the parts that many people may not know you love. He knows, and He wants you to know that He can share it all with you. All of it.

I once had a dream in which the first words I heard from Jesus in heaven were that He loved to throw a football! That might make you laugh, but you have to know that there is nothing on this earth I love more than playing catch with a football. I will do it for hours with my guys. We run patterns and pretend we are quarterbacks barking out plays over a make believe line. So what those simple words meant to me is that I have a God who really "gets" me and wants to enjoy life right beside me.

Now the words you most want to hear from Jesus may not be about how tight the spiral is on his football pass. You may want to know that He can garden with you or make those spreadsheets come out right in a way that just makes you exhale in satisfaction. Maybe you long for Him to sit down and figure out the last couple of words on that crossword with you, or just sit and take in an amazing sunset. He can do all those things. We have a Redeemer so personal that He knows what we love more than we do. And this is the best part: He wants to do it with us!

He wants to live my life right beside me! He wants to live life right beside you! Did you hear that? He wants to live beside you! If there is a common thread I can trace through the stories I have listened to from hundreds of women, it is that they are lonely. Whether they are sitting on a rugged bench at a retreat or across from me at my desk or even beside me in a grocery store line, telling me bits and pieces of their stories, the words I always hear at some point are "I am so lonely."

Those words are almost always accompanied by these, "No one really understands me or knows my feelings and dreams." Wherever you are reading this book – at your house, at your desk, or outside in that very nice quiet spot in your yard – I hope you can escape your setting for a moment, put you life on pause, and just stop and think about the last time you felt alone, misunderstood, desperate.

When was it? Possibly you were in the middle of a crowd—and yet all alone. Maybe you were washing dishes with a family around you, yet no one noticed the tears you wiped away as you stood there with the weight of the world on your shoulders. Maybe it was last night, as you struggled to go to sleep in a lonely, empty house. As you started the same movie from the beginning, set the sleep timer of your television to go off so that, until it did, you would have noise to drown out another night of silence, another night filled with thoughts you did not want. When was it?

Even in that place of loneliness there was someone with you. As you cried silent tears no one saw, there was a hand willing to wipe them away. Do you know you have a Redeemer? A Savior? One who loves you so much He would stop at nothing to redeem your life? Jesus knows everything you would ever think, everything you would ever dream, everything you would ever do, both the good and the bad. He knows it all, He took it, and then He picked it all up—the pain, the loneliness, the lost dreams and hopes, the sin, the sorrow. He carried those things on bruised and beaten shoulders to the top of a hill and died for them. He died so you would never have to feel alone, He died so that the deepest desires of your heart for relationship would be met perfectly in Him. He died to give you hope, He died to bring you life, and most of all, He died to set you free.

In Galatians 5 the Apostle Paul says it in the best and simplest way: "It is for freedom that He set you free."² Freedom to live a full and meaningful life, freedom from the pain of lost dreams and hopes. Freedom from the guilt that our failures bring, freedom from expectations that destroy us and rob us of joy. Freedom to play the game the way it was created to be, to play hours of catch, to share the deepest, most secret places of our hearts with the One who created us to utter those words to no one else but Him.

What have you been keeping from Him? What does He know but still needs you to admit? What places have you hidden from Him because you were afraid that even He would not care? That's not true. Our relationship with Him is the most intimate we will ever have. What is stopping you? He has been right there all along.

IN THE GARDEN

I had one of those moments with God several years ago. It was in the months after my divorce, a year when many emotions were so raw and were more real than I had ever felt them before. I had been reading and studying and came to a place where I just wanted to have it out with God. I wanted to lay all the cards on the table and see what He would do if I talked to Him about all the pain I felt—not only for what had just taken place in my family, but for everything. All forty years of it, the good, the bad, and the really, really ugly parts.

So I took my journal and began tracing my life from as far back as I could remember, the parts that hurt me, the parts I knew must have hurt Him. The parts I would never understand, the disappointing parts, and the parts that were too wonderful and amazing to believe, even as I looked back on them. Page after page, I wrote for several hours while on my knees beside my bed. I was often in tears, often angry, but always honest. As I got to the end of my time, writing out and owning every important moment I could remember, I began to scribble the chorus of one of my favorite old hymns, "In the Garden."

> And He walks with me,
> And He talks with me,
> And He tells me I am His own,

And the joy we share as we tarry there,
None other has ever known.[3]

As I lifted my pen from the paper after having written that last word, the truth of what I had just experienced finally came over me.

Those moments I just wrote about, I had lived with God, but very few of them had I actually shared with Him. Many of the tough times I had just gutted out somehow, the best I could. But as He quietly reminded me of the words of that old hymn, He also spoke truth to the depths of my heart. "Becky, I have been missing you. In fact, I have been missing something that no one else can give me, for the joy we share is so unique that no one else can know it the same way."

God created us to be most ourselves in His presence. He is most glorified in us when we are living completely in Him. Living fully in Him was what was lacking in those many years of loneliness and pain, in the darkness of a life spent in agony for the choices being made around me, for the choices I made, and for the choices God made. But now, in the middle of the famine I could know complete love, complete hope, complete freedom through my relationship with my Redeemer. I could ask Him for the secrets, for the cheats that would open the door to a whole new level of living. That is what a redeemer does. I do not have to wait for heaven; I can know that closeness, intimacy, hope, and joy today, living life right beside Him. It does not matter if you are a man or a woman, single or married, young or old, fat or skinny, dark or light. We all have the same needs, and all our needs can be met at the feet of our Redeemer.

So how do you do that? How do you go to your Redeemer to meet the struggles, challenges, and famines of your life? Let's look back at our story and get some ideas on how to approach our Redeemer when we take a look at how Ruth approached hers.

RUTH'S REDEEMER

Naomi and Ruth have been living pretty well off all that Ruth has been able to gather behind the workers at Boaz' field. But now the harvest is coming to a close, and Naomi wisely begins to look ahead to the challenges before them. This hand-to-mouth existence will not keep them through the long winter months. The survival living they have been used to over the last many years will not provide a future for young Ruth or a chance for Naomi to enjoy grandchildren.

Wise Naomi had lived through so much loss and pain. She had experienced famine and death, and she had been stuck in a foreign land, but she had also been determined even in her bitterness and anger to come back home. After all that uphill living, she was ready to experience life in a different way. She had shown hope at earlier times in her life; it had sustained her in Moab and brought her to the long trip home. Now that hope was being turned into action as she looked for ways to open doors in order to make way for someone to redeem their lives.

A kinsman-redeemer was a built-in provision for the people of Israel. When someone died, a near relative from the dead person's family would come forward and take care of the remaining members of the family. This would include purchasing their land, and in the case of Ruth and Naomi, the redeemer would also take Ruth to be his wife and provide children through her so that the dead man's name would continue in Israel. Quite a responsibility. Quite a provision.

Armed with this knowledge, Naomi made a plan. As would be part of any love story montage, Naomi helped Ruth choose the finest of her clothes and did an ancient version of the modern day makeover. Ruth, who was already very beautiful, needed to look her best for the one opportunity Naomi saw to demonstrate to Boaz both their need and his opportunity. Until this point he had simply shown them kindness, but now Naomi saw the perfect scenario in place to help him understand his greater responsibility toward the two women.

THE PLAN

The right opportunity came at the end of the harvest, the time when the men threshed the barley on the community threshing floor. This event was something like a celebration at the end of a physically demanding harvest season. Once the barley was threshed, there was a party that included some eating and drinking. Afterward all the tired men would pull out their sleeping bags and camp out on the threshing floor. Naomi was well aware of this event, and she saw it as just the right time for Ruth to disclose to Boaz their near-relative relationship, thus allowing him to know how they needed him to come to their aid as their redeemer.

So the plan was set. Boaz would be at the threshing floor and Ruth would be looking her best. The love story is in full motion. You could cue the soft music in the background as the beautiful Ruth quietly approaches the unsuspecting Boaz who is asleep on the threshing floor. The plan called for Ruth to lie at his feet and await his instructions. Ruth did exactly that, although it must have been awkward, to say the least, for her to lie there until he woke up. This was not a normal practice, so she was depending greatly on his generosity and kindness. Women just did not go around sleeping at the feet of men, especially on the threshing floor, surrounded by all the other men of the town.

But it did not take long before something woke Boaz and he realized someone was there. He was surprised to find Ruth, but his surprise turned to joy as she made her request of him. She asked him to cover her with his blanket. Ruth was certainly saying more here than that she was cold in the middle of the night. The act of covering someone in that culture reflected a willingness to protect and provide. In the case of Ruth, she was asking Boaz to do even more than that; she was asking him to be her husband.

It was not an easy middle-of-the-night request to respond to. But Boaz, always the gentlemen, reacts in a gracious, kind way. His response shows not only delight, but also insight. He is thrilled that she would make this request of him and also aware that it is not a sure thing. Boaz must have known of his near relative status to Ruth, but had assumed that, because she had not asked him before, she was looking for one of the younger men in town to show interest in her. He knew that although he was a near relative, there was one person more closely related to Ruth. Possibly one of Elimelech's brothers was still alive, and by law he had the first choice to redeem the property as well as to take on the responsibilities of the dead relative.

Even though he voices this concern in his response, there is no change in his desire to care for her. His words to her are full of kindness and a will to help. In every way he allows her to know that she has done all that is required of her; he will care for the rest of the details. And instead of asking her to leave, he encourages her to stay there at his feet, covered by his blanket, until morning. The night was not a safe time for a woman to be walking around, but the other reality was that it would not be safe either for her to be found there at Boaz' feet in the morning. So before first light she woke up and prepared to leave. However, Boaz would not let her go empty handed. He filled her shawl with fresh barley and sent her home full of hope as well as with provisions to give to her mother-in-law.

Cool story, is it not? Can't you imagine it as a movie? It would make for a very sweet love story. You could almost picture the montage where they are shown falling in love more and more each day, as beautiful, penniless, yet determined Ruth goes to the field of the handsome and generous Boaz. Hollywood could do a great job with this one. But as much as we would all love a wholesome love story where the right guy gets the girl, we can learn much more from this little encounter than how these two people fell in love. We can learn how we can fall in love with our Redeemer every single day. We can learn to approach Him, to lie at His feet, to ask for His covering and protection, and most of all, we can learn to walk away full of His hope, His promises, and His peace.

APPROACHING OUR REDEEMER

As Ruth crept up to the blanketed form of Boaz in the far corner of the threshing floor that night, she must have done so with more than a little anxiety. It was a bold move for her to risk lying at his feet in the hope he would redeem her life and cover her with his protection and provision. Ruth was anxious not only because she was demonstrating her plight to a man; the deeper truth was that she must have been anxious because she truly had needs, deep and real ones, needs that would not go away unless this man responded.

When we approach our Redeemer we need to know the same thing. Our needs may make so much racket as we approach that everyone on the threshing floor can hear them. Or they may be more secret, and no one would ever guess there are places in our hearts that only our Redeemer could enter. In either case, it takes a tremendous amount of courage to acknowledge our needs not only in our minds, but also in our spirits, as we shuffle across the threshing floor to our Redeemer.

There must have been a desperate quality in Ruth that night that would have been attractive to Boaz. Not a pleading quality as much as an honest acknowledgement of her own needs and her understanding that he alone could meet them. That would have made her all the more beautiful as she lay there, hopefully staring up at him that night. That acknowledgment is exactly what makes us irresistible to God when we come to Him with those places in our lives we cannot fix. Possibly we have tried for some time to make them right, and now, tired and discouraged, we finally drag ourselves to the feet of our Redeemer, weary beyond belief from the journey, almost afraid to hope that He will want to do something for us. But first we must make the request. We must ask Him to meet our needs with the simple question, "Lord, will you cover me?"

What does it do to your heart, your mind, or your spirit when you ask someone for help? I can tell you what it has always done to mine. It makes me feel like a failure. Why is that? What makes it hard for us to reach out and allow someone else to know we need them?

Maybe it's that American will and self-reliance that we are always so proud of. Possibly it's that no one has ever seemed to want to offer us help in the past. Maybe we have asked, hoped, waited, but in the end the task to fix what is wrong always falls on us. Possibly the core of what makes it hard to ask for help is summed up in one simple word, pride.

If the antonym to pride is humility, it must then mean that in order to make a request you must first be humble enough to acknowledge that you cannot do something on your own, that you truly need the help of another. Boone had no trouble grabbing that laptop to access the help he knew was waiting on the internet. There was no pride left; he had no confidence that he had the answers. But he did know the right questions, and he knew just who to ask—the creator of the game. That is all we have to do. Go to our Creator and ask Him for help.

Ruth's simple request took tremendous humility, but she was a humble woman. Her life had been an ongoing process of developing humility. The painful days when she was first a widow, the tiring days on her long journey to Bethlehem, the exhausting days gathering barley behind the harvesters—all this produced humility in Ruth. Yet, in a deeper sense I do not believe Ruth had ever been a prideful person, thus necessitating the lessons of humility she lived out. No, that was not the reason. Ruth was humble because that is the way we take when we truly want to show godly character. Jesus was humbled to the point of death, even death on a cross;[4] yet He was without sin and without pride, not even a trace. So to be humbled is to be like Christ.

Humility is an amazing character quality that, although hard to attain, will benefit us in ways that exceed our imagination. Not only does it allow us to enlist the help of others as we move through our lives; it also gives us the immeasurable gift of a soft heart. At countless moments in our journey, a single choice will give us one of two outcomes—a softening or hardening of our hearts. Without question, when God says He wants to recapture our hearts, He is talking about humble, pliable hearts. He needs to work with them a lot like a potter who is working clay into what He desires. And let me tell you, the moment that request for covering is out of our mouths, He begins the forming process.

THE POTTER'S WHEEL

I spent a good period of time during my high school years in ceramics class. There were at least two reasons for that. The first was that I enjoyed working with clay very much. The second reason almost rivaled the first in importance: the class was taught by my basketball coach, a man I enjoyed learning from. I also, quite honestly, believed he would give me a favorable grade.

As I moved from beginning to advanced ceramics over my time in school, I learned a variety of ways to work with clay. At first I worked with it on a broad, dry table, using only my hands to form and shape that gray material into wonderful teapots, bookends, bowls, and vases, many of which ended up wrapped as gifts for my mom. Several of those "masterpieces" continue to take up residence at my parents' home.

During my second year of ceramics, I was introduced to the wheel. The first day was messy in every possible way. The wheel was motored by your foot and consisted of a metal disk with a small lip to protect you from the spray of the clay-water mixture that whipped off the rapidly turning wheel. You sat on a small bench behind the disk with an apron covering your clothes and patiently worked the clay as it spun around the wheel. My time on the wheel was short-lived, however, as I quickly learned that I did not have the touch to work with clay in that form. So I returned happily to the table, where the work was slower and more controlled.

But the days when the students working on the wheel learned a new concept, we all came and watched as our teacher masterfully worked with the clay. He began with a healthy chunk about the size of a misshapen softball. The first step was always to center it on the wheel. For this, my teacher slowly started the wheel spinning and gently pressed the moistened clay up and down until it became a perfectly circular mound spinning in perfect symmetry with the wheel. Next, he carefully pressed his fingers into the center of the mound, pulling outward as he pressed down. As the wheel continued to turn at just the right speed, his hands worked the clay gently into a perfectly round bowl, vase, or cup. When the wheel finally came to rest, you could see the result of what skillful workmanship can do with a soft, misshapen lump of clay.

Maybe that is exactly how you feel as you tentatively approach your Redeemer today—like a lump of clay good for almost nothing. But let me ask you, are you a soft lump of clay or a dry, cracked mound so hardened by life that you stare at Him, daring Him to find a speck of softness in you? You can never ask Him to cover you that way. In that form you can never expect Him to recapture your heart, to work you into the masterpiece He dreams of. No, you must be soft, and that is all. You don't have to be complete, finished, or smooth. Softness is all that is required. He will do the rest. He will cover you with His skillful, kind, gentle hands and do the rest.

Can you do that? Can you approach your Redeemer with expectancy, hope, and nothing else? Can you with humility and softness of heart simply ask Him to cover you? If you cannot, maybe you need to check back on chapter five and take a more honest look at some of the struggles of your life, some of the deaths and famines. Honesty may be loud and messy, but it yields an amazingly soft heart, one that is willing not only to be formed, directed, covered, and protected, but most of all, recaptured!

STAY UNTIL MORNING

Okay, so humble, soft-hearted Ruth breathlessly asks Boaz to cover her. What is his response? He is more than thrilled to do it. He lets her know he has a plan; it is all settled. All that Ruth needs to do is run home and give Naomi the good news. They will be redeemed, they are rescued, they will have enough barley not only for the winter, but for the rest of their lives. There will be a wedding. There will need to be planning. Romance is in full bloom. Things are finally going right. Time to celebrate.

But that is not all that happens. As soon as Boaz finishes telling her what he will do, he instructs her to stay put. Do you know why? Because it is still dark. Remember, this is the era of the Judges, a time of unparalleled unrest and violence in Israel. There might be dangerous men out at night, possibly even some animals that might harm her. No, the safest place for Ruth is with Boaz. Isn't that cool! What is any good love story without some potential danger from which the hero is willing to protect the beautiful, desperate woman? Well, that may be a bit over the top, but the truth is simple: it is not safe to be running around in the dark, and Boaz is concerned.

Now you probably have not been to any threshing floors in the middle of the night lately—or ever, for that matter—but I am almost certain you have known dark times in your life. We all know darkness in some form, and even when we dare to hope for something new in the morning, a gift exactly like the one Boaz had given Ruth, there is this reality that darkness is not a safe time to do anything.

However, sometimes we ignore warnings and go out in the dark anyway, often with very bad results. When we have had the courage and humility to approach our Redeemer, when we have heard His loving reply to our request for His covering, followed by His loving, kind, and wise direction to stay at His feet until it is again light, there are times when we think we can go out in the darkness anyway. We think we are ready for anything; after all, didn't we just hear from God Himself that He would take care of everything? Can't we move out and just jump back into the light? There are some good hours being wasted here! We need to get back to life, get busy, get productive, be back in charge!

I have plowed out into many a dark night, trying to take on the world with only hope and have found myself quickly falling flat. It is not enough just to be willing to lie down at the foot of our Redeemer; no, we really need to stay there. We need to wait until it is light to get back to life with its methodically relentless pace.

I can tell you for a fact that after my divorce there were, for me, years of darkness that contained limited, at times zero energy for anything but functioning at the most rudimentary level. Looking back on those years, I now see I truly was lying at the feet of my Redeemer, protecting and providing for my boys' needs, but doing little else. At the time, I remember thinking I was failing miserably in not having the energy to keep my house in order, to keep the laundry up, or to get creative meals on the table. I was shocked to see how I had let myself go, gaining weight, caring very little about how I looked or dressed. It was dark outside, and I was simply lying at the feet of my Redeemer. I see it now as a valuable time of loving and sharing life with my sons. We had nights where we set up our tent in the house and cooked s'mores—and woke up to the empty packages still on the floor.

We laugh about some of those days now, but back then I was less than thrilled at what I viewed as a total lack of motivation. The reality today is that my house is cleaner that it has ever been, my cooking is back to whatever level of mediocrity it used to show, and I even take time now and then to exercise and do my nails. It has all come back, and do you know why? Because it is now light. The light came back in layers, slowly, steadily, in a sustainable way for not only me, but for my guys as well.

Now each time I find myself in darkness I know two things. First, it will not last forever. And second, I cannot function at my normal pace when it is dark. Just think of how it is when you are out at night without a flashlight, when every step needs to be taken carefully, slowly, with purpose. Life needs to be lived like that at times.

I don't know about you, but I still have dark times; my life is not flooded by constant light. However, I have learned to handle the darkness better. Its duration is shorter, my expectations have lessened, and the biggest change is that I spend that time more quietly, more still. I spend more of the dark times at the foot of my Redeemer. It is a lot safer there, and the time goes by so much faster.

I am learning to almost predict when those moments of darkness might come. I am single, and holidays are very different than they used to be. On the occasions when I do not spend them with my guys, I often find myself right smack dab in the middle of the darkness. I know I can help that time pass by planning ahead and making sure I spend it with people I enjoy or doing things I like doing, rather than sitting at home alone, feeling depressed. I am learning, though, that I am not great at it yet. But I know one thing for sure: when He tells me to stay until morning I listen, because the darkness is not safe, and it's no place to be trying to find your way home. There is nothing like waiting at the feet of your Redeemer as you watch the first rays of light break through the darkness.

LEAVE FULL

Morning came for Ruth that day at the threshing floor, and as she noiselessly prepared to leave, Boaz must have quietly called her back. He wanted her to leave full. I am sure she was full of hope and full of good news she could hardly wait to tell Naomi about, but in addition to the intangible things that were stirring in her heart, Boaz wanted her to take something with her that she could actually see and hold onto. So he filled her apron with fresh barley from the harvest and sent her on her way. Ruth, who just hours before had come to him carrying a very heavy burden, now left with the energy and hope characteristic of one whose burden has been lifted. The only thing weighing her down was generous provision, a small down payment toward what would be a lifetime of fullness.

How can you and I leave full after spending time at the feet of our Redeemer? Without question, the easiest and clearest way to do that is to not pick up the burden you left at His feet to begin with. To leave not full of your problems, your fears, your doubts, your struggles, but instead full of His promises, His provisions, His hope, His plans, His dreams for your life. Basically, you leave all of you there, and you leave full of Him.

That sounds really great, doesn't it? Who would not want to leave with arms overflowing with God's promises and dreams for your life? Well, you and I for starters. We leave without those promises and dreams for us all the time. Do you remember the homeless man back in Chapter one who left the generous man holding a bag full of the very thing he needed (food) in order to beg someone else for it? No, it is definitely harder than it sounds to leave full from the presence of our Redeemer, but it is not impossible.

In order for you to leave Him fully satisfied, something first must happen that truly convinces you to make a change in both your thinking and your actions. Coming to your Redeemer is an act of surrender. Do you remember that you have a need you cannot meet? You are asking for help. Now this is where the proverbial "rubber meets the road." Will you take the help being offered? What if that help does not take the form you thought it would? What if that help does not give you something you were dreaming of? What if that help means you have to change some of the ways you are living? Will you do it in order to leave full? If you answer with a resounding "YES," I will not believe you; neither should you.

Instead, if you give me a solid "I would sure like to," I think we have a place to start. If you want to know where to start, you must begin with what you are convinced of. What do you truly believe in? Have you ever thought of that? Not the things you wish were true or want to be true, but what do you actually believe is true down to the core? Because what you believe to be true will without question be the thing that directs your choices.

Like most people, I am sure you believe you need food and water in some form every day to survive. Because you believe that, you make sure you regularly eat something. We often take in just a little more than we need, but that has more to do with our appetites and lack of self-control than our beliefs. We also find time each day to sleep, because we sense that our bodies are slowing down and believe sleep will energize us.

Now comes the interesting part. For most of us, the above things are pretty much mandatory. All people have those basic needs and address them in some form each day in order to sustain life. But what else do you do? What else do you believe, what else are you totally convinced you have to do in order to really live?

For some, exercise is part of that routine. Such people are convinced that in order to help their bodies function at the highest and most enjoy-able level they must have an ongoing exercise plan. Others are forced to regularly exercise because of health issues. Still others may exercise not for their health or how their body feels, but for how their body looks. For the sake of argument, let's focus on this last group.

If it helps, I will begin by confessing that I have been part of that one for most of my life. The problem behind this motivation for exercising is that you can never truly leave full because you are dependent on someone else telling you that you are okay. And as you and I have learned in life, that method is less than dependable. So the key is then to take away the external motivation and turn it into something you do because you are convinced that you will feel better, live longer, avoid diseases, and generally enjoy life more when you are healthy—which requires some level of exercise. Easier said then done; I am with you on that.

But think for a moment about God's purpose of redeeming us, of recapturing hearts. It is not just for His benefit, but also for ours. Remember, He knows what is coming; He is the One who created us. He knows all about the struggles we are going to face, the famines, the dry, dusty fields. He alone knows the clues that will unlock the encouragement we need to move through hard times, stuck places. He knows we need those days when we come bursting into the house with armloads of grain to offset the days when all we took in was an eyeful of withered stalks.

Energy is one of the things He wants us to leave full of. A great way to build energy is through exercise. He also wants us to leave hopeful, and a great way to do that is to believe in what we do not see. He wants us to leave encouraged; often the only way to do that is to intentionally think about truth. He wants our hearts, and the only way He could have them is to redeem them. Are you going to let Him?

So what did you do today? I am guessing you woke up after several hours of sleep, ate something, and most likely brushed your teeth. The rest is up for grabs. Did you take a jog, a vitamin, did you spend time reading something that would encourage you? Those, too, are choices, but making them consistently over time for no other reason than that they would be just plain good for you is very healing and healthy and generally will leave you feeling full—in a good way! They will leave you at the feet of your Redeemer with a heart safely in His hands and with an armful of hope to dump onto your kitchen table.

ALL THAT IS NEEDED

Ruth has rested at the foot of the redeemer who has assured her he will do all she needs, and as she unloads her apron full of barley on the table in front of Naomi and recounts her story, she is again reminded of the truth. Boaz will do the rest. Naomi told Ruth to relax; Boaz will not rest until he has done all that is needed to make sure they are redeemed.

Wow, what a sigh of relief Ruth could let out as she fell elated but exhausted onto a chair. As the realization of what was happening swept over her I am certain this godly woman was filled with incredible peace and hope. She had done her part; now the rest was up to someone else, someone stronger than her, someone who had greater resources and the ability to alter her circumstances. Someone who would love and care for her. He would do all that was needed.

Do you know that today? Do you know that truth as you face the daylight of your life right now? Do you know there is Someone bigger, stronger, and more capable than you who is for you, loves you, and will redeem your life? There is! And the great thing is that He loves you and knows what is best for you. He not only wants to give you the answers; He wants to live life out beside you. Playing catch, watching the sunset, quilting, shopping, reading. Whatever He created you to love He wants to enjoy right beside you.

He has already done the hard part, but we have our parts, too. Ruth needed to go to the threshing floor that night, she needed to approach her redeemer, she had to ask for his covering, she had to choose to stay put until morning, and when the light came, she had to leave with his provision instead of the heavy burden she came with. That finished, the rest was up to Boaz. Once you approach your Redeemer the same way, the rest is up to Him.

Aren't you so glad that God takes care of what we could never do? Aren't you so thankful that once we do our parts, small by comparison, He takes care of the rest? I, for one, am very grateful for that. My dreams, thoughts, and hopes are way too small. If it were left up to my plans and abilities, my life would be dull, boring, and colorless. But that is not the case. I am simply to do my part and then have the audacity to dream His dreams, think His thoughts, and live out His plans. That is exciting in every single way! It changes the way you live, it changes what you want, and most of all, it changes how you pray.

I used to pray for the regular things everyone prayed for. Things that possibly might happen whether God showed up or not. Things that seemed a little more doable for God; after all, some didn't even seem to require supernatural intervention. Just the normal course of life would provide the desired outcome. It sort of boosts your prayer life to see the answers come so effortlessly; it's a lot like starting a "to do" list with several things you have already finished, in order to get you going. But it's not an advisable way to live, dream, or certainly pray.

No, letting God do the rest requires bold faith and even more radical prayers. The greatest prayer I have ever heard was uttered by Joshua as he led Israel on a headfirst assault on the nations in the Promised Land. Before he led his men to fight the Amorites, he was given a pledge from God that he would have total victory. Fueled by that word, he led his troops into an amazing battle that raged all day and into the night. So sure was Joshua of God's promise, so full was he after time at the feet of his Redeemer that in the midst of battle he cried out this bold prayer: he asked God to hold the sun in the sky until the battle was won for Israel.[5]

Now that was not a little prayer! He did not ask just for victory or limited casualties or even for fair weather conditions, for God had already pelted the enemy with a hailstorm. No, Joshua's prayer called for God to be God; it was the kind of prayer only God could answer. He was in essence saying, I have done my part; now, God, you take it from here, but let's make it memorable. And it was truly memorable, because God answered his prayer as the sun stood still in the sky until the battle was won. What a vote of confidence for Joshua's leadership, what a clear indication of his faith!

Are you willing to do that? Are you willing to sit like Ruth in relaxed confidence that you have done your part, and leave the rest to God? People who are convinced of God's power and provision for them, people who have spent the darkness at the foot of their Redeemer can do that. They pray prayers only God can answer, they dream dreams only God can be in. They live life in intimate closeness with their Redeemer, the One who gave everything to walk through life right beside them.

He Comes to Where You Are

Redemption is a simple term we use in many ways. What it basically means is to buy back. A redemption center is where you pick up whatever you have gotten. To redeem a coupon is a great deal for the one receiving the value, but the only way you can do that is if someone else is willing to pay the difference. Marketers for major companies do the math and come up with a solid fiscal reason for issuing the coupon. But it remains that if it is to be redeemed it will ultimately have to cost someone something.

For the consumer with coupon in hand, all you really know is that the amount of money you brought was enough, because someone else will make up the difference between what something costs and what you are willing to pay for it. Another way to look at it is to say that someone comes to where you are and is willing to pay the difference.

I learned this in a most unusual way several years ago. I have already told you that Sandy and I made a commitment to study the Bible. That commitment has been the reason we have continued to do so for so many years now. I guarded it very closely and took more than a little pride in the fact that we had never missed a week. Sure, I fell behind a few times when life got overwhelming, yet I had always been able to catch up. But each time I told someone about how to study Scripture, I felt it was so important to be able to say that this was the one place in my life I would never miss. Well, I found out that what I really couldn't miss was the lesson of grace God would teach me through my friend.

I had fallen behind in my study one spring, not just a few chapters behind, but quite a few weeks worth of chapters, maybe even a month. One day Sandy approached me about it and simply told me it was okay to take a break if I needed it, and when I caught up to where she was, we could continue from there. After all, what is another month when you are studying for over eleven years!

I thought this suggestion was very kind of her. I thanked her and promised I would make a plan to catch up within a week when we would be back on track. She assured me it was okay to take my time; the important thing was that we were studying, not the speed at which we finished. But even with Sandy's admonition that I need not hurry ringing in my ears, that night I went home and plotted how many chapters I would have to do each day to finish in the shortest amount of time. Needless to say, I felt so defeated with all my planning that I didn't even have the energy to do a single chapter.

The next day I came into the office, and Sandy told me that as she was praying about our studying, God gave her a new plan. She would come back to where I was, restudy those chapters, and we would be right on schedule. I was no longer behind. Wow, what a picture of grace, what a new understanding of the role of a redeemer not only to buy you back, but more importantly, to come back to where you are and walk beside you to where you should go!

When Jesus died on the cross He became the Redeemer of all mankind. In one sweeping act He walked back to all of us and essentially said, "If you will accept my sacrifice to cover your sins, you are no longer behind; you are right where you are supposed to be." That is grace, undeserved and amazing and as simple as it can be. But how wonderful to the core.

A redeemer taps into your greatest longings, a place deeper than any spouse, friend, or child can reach. The place in all of us that desires to be fully known not by another person, but by the One who created us. What are you waiting for? He is your Creator, your Redeemer, the One who not only made your heart but will do anything to recapture it. What could be better? He not only wants to play catch with a football; he can give you the secret to the game. He made you, He knows what you love, and guess what? He loves it, too!

Chapter Eight

Better

—⁂—

*Meanwhile Boaz went up to the town gate and sat there. When the
kinsman-redeemer he had mentioned came along, Boaz said, "Come
over here, my friend, and sit down." So he went over and sat down.*

*Boaz took ten of the elders of the town and said, "Sit here," and
they did so. Then he said to the kinsman-redeemer, "Naomi, who has
come back from Moab, is selling the piece of land that belonged to
our brother Elimelech. I thought I should bring the matter to your
attention and suggest that you buy it in the presence of these seated
here and in the presence of the elders of my people. If you will redeem
it, do so. But if you will not, tell me, so I will know. For no one has
the right to do it except you, and I am next in line."*

"I will redeem it," he said.

*Then Boaz said, "On the day you buy the land from Naomi
and from Ruth the Moabitess, you acquire the dead man's widow,
in order to maintain the name of the dead with his property."*

*At this, the kinsman-redeemer said, "Then I cannot redeem it
because I might endanger my own estate. You redeem it yourself. I
cannot do it." (Now in earlier times in Israel, for the redemption
and transfer of property to become final, one party took off his
sandal and gave it to the other. This was the method of legalizing*

transactions in Israel.) So the kinsman-redeemer said to Boaz, "Buy it yourself." And he removed his sandal.

Then Boaz announced to the elders and all the people, "Today you are witnesses that I have bought from Naomi all the property of Elimelech, Kilion and Mahlon. I have also acquired Ruth the Moabitess, Mahlon's widow, as my wife, in order to maintain the name of the dead with his property, so that his name will not disappear from among his family or from the town records. Today you are witnesses!" Then the elders and all those at the gate said, "We are witnesses. May the Lord make the woman who is coming into your home like Rachel and Leah, who together built up the house of Israel. May you have standing in Ephrathah and be famous in Bethlehem. Through the offspring the Lord gives you by this young woman, may your family be like that of Perez, whom Tamar bore to Judah."

So Boaz took Ruth and she became his wife. Then he went to her, and the Lord enabled her to conceive, and she gave birth to a son. The women said to Naomi: "Praise be to the Lord, who this day has not left you without a kinsman-redeemer. May he become famous throughout Israel! He will renew your life and sustain you in your old age. For your daughter-in-law, who loves you and who is better to you than seven sons, has given him birth."

Then Naomi took the child, laid him in her lap and cared for him. The women living there said, "Naomi has a son." And they named him Obed. He was the father of Jesse, the father of David.

This, then, is the family line of Perez:
Perez was the father of Hezron,
Hezron the father of Ram,
Ram the father of Amminadab,
Amminadab the father of Nahshon,
Nahshon the father of Salmon,
Salmon the father of Boaz,
Boaz the father of Obed,
Obed the father of Jesse,
and Jesse the father of David.[1]

LEGOS

AS THE MOM of four boys I can tell you I have become somewhat of an expert on Legos. My sons have literally had tens of thousands of those little bricks of all different shapes and sizes, and I have to tell you I love them as much as they do. I love every part of building them, from laying out all the pieces and seeing the cool shaped ones you will work with to opening the thick book of directions.

Lego directions are awesome; they are so clear, and each page builds on the last one. As you turn to a fresh page you are shown what you have already built, then you are told which pieces to add, where to put them. And the best part of a brand new set of Legos is that you know that in the box you have every single piece required for building the object on the cover. There is nothing to hinder you from creating your own Lego masterpiece just like the one pictured.

My boys all knew that the day after Christmas and their birthdays would be reserved for building Legos. The piles of other toys and boxes still littered the floor, but space at the center of the dining room table was always reserved for Lego building. We loved each and every second as we searched through piles of plastic bricks to find just the right one for the next section of the project. We even created our own language for use between the one who built and the one who searched. "Double fat eight gray" meant that I needed a gray piece that was not the wafer-thin kind and had two sets of rows of four circles each. Pretty amazing, huh? Suffice it to say, we took Lego building very seriously! Nothing compared to the feeling of turning to the last few pages of the directions and finishing our set to make it look exactly like the one on the cover.

We have built many sets since my oldest son Trev turned four and we learned how to build Legos together. But it was not until Christmas of that same year that we received the coolest Lego set ever, the Pirate Ship. My college-age son will tell you to this day that the Pirate Ship was the best Lego ever made. That Pirate Ship took us two days to build. Fortunately I had two days to do nothing but build a Lego set with him, because I was very pregnant with his triplet brothers.

That pirate ship was a masterpiece, and everything about it was truly amazing, from the bright red cannons that moved back and forth on the deck to the masts with the skull and crossbones on them. The ship even had pirate flags on the top of each mast; it was a thing of beauty. As we put the last piece in place, we both celebrated. Our set looked just like the picture on the front of the box. We even made sure that each pirate was exactly in his spot. Let me tell you, we focused on every detail. If the Captain's peg leg was lifted up in the picture, you can be sure our pirate held the exact same pose! We loved Legos!!

But it does not matter how great the Lego sets are or how closely they resemble the picture on the front of the box. The thing about Legos is that they don't stay together. And you know what else? Those pieces are very small, are easily lost or vacuumed up, and each one is important for the whole set. Over the next months and eventually years, the pirate ship began to fall apart. It broke apart each time it fell off a shelf or ended up in the hands of one of his toddler brothers who had no idea as to the treasure he held.

With each break, our old Pirate Ship was harder and harder to put together. It was not for lack of effort; we really tried. Each and every time it broke apart, Trev came to me with tears of despair filling his eyes, and we did our best to rebuild it. But the problem was that, as a result of the break, we no longer had all the pieces. The directions no longer worked, because we simply did not have what was necessary to put it back together. And so it was with great sorrow that one day we made the decision to put all the remaining pieces of the pirate ship in the huge overflowing Lego box, the container that held the broken pieces of other precious treasures that had ended the same way: a castle, a village, an island, and sadly, even the western outpost Fort Legorado.

But you know, an amazing thing has happened to our huge Lego box with all the tens of thousands of stray pieces that once belonged to a set. After all these years it still gets dumped out on a big blanket and played with. In fact, on some days we sit on the floor and create all kinds of amazing things with the broken pieces. When we find the pieces of the pirate ship, we turn them over in our hands, giving them a long look, remembering the part they had played in what once was a very cool ship. Then we put them together with parts of the old fort and castle to make a kind of ship-castle-outpost-hotel-looking thing with a pirate flag on top. It is really quite amazing. Is it as good as the pirate ship? No, it's different. It's new, it's creative, and it was fun to build. Our new creation required no directions, no order, no picture on the box lid to follow, just complete freedom to create what only we can imagine.

A New Picture

Our lives can be a bit that way at times. We carefully build our dreams, following the typical directions and order. All the pieces seem to be in place for the perfect life, and we love it. Then, all of a sudden things begin to happen, things get broken, important things, precious things. And even with our best effort to build them back, sometimes the pieces are no longer there to make it look like it did before. You cannot make it look like the picture on the box, and the directions no longer work because you simply don't have all the pieces. At those times you can feel like you are just a bunch of broken pieces, pushed aside, unwanted, unloved, with no purpose, no hope.

When my boys came to me heartbroken with a former masterpiece in pieces, I typically said, "You know the great thing about Lego creations, guys, is that they were made to be rebuilt, they were designed to be broken, recreated. There are no boundaries to what you can do; you can build whatever you can think of."

That is so true of our lives. When we come to God with the broken pieces of our life and in tears ask Him, "What are we to do now?" we wonder how in the world it can be built back to what it used to be. At those times, He lovingly reminds us that life is about being broken. Life is about being rebuilt. I believe each time we drop the broken pieces of our life into His hands, what He most wants us to know is that He is Creator God. He is our Redeemer; He wants to use even the broken and shattered pieces of our lives to recapture our hearts. He has a new plan, and the picture on the box top no longer applies. That dream may have died, but He has a new dream in His mind. He will use not only the pieces you have brought to him; He will find more. He will blend the broken pieces of your life into something new, something amazing, something only He could create, something only He can see. Because He has His own picture of what our lives are supposed to look like.

Do you have anything that is broken in your life? Maybe something you love has fallen off the shelf and is now in a heap on the floor, unrecognizable. Maybe someone else has broken your dreams, and the pieces are gone. Or maybe as you read these words, your heart is in your throat because you know that your most precious dream is broken because of you. You were the one who made the choices that caused life to fall apart for you.

If your life feels a bit broken, you are in good company. Many of us have pieces of our lives lying all around us. Some things are broken from our own choices, some from the choices of others. And some of them just plain fell to the ground because our lives can be pretty shaky at times. What matters now is what you are going to do with all those pieces. Will you throw them away because you can't seem to build back the dreams you wanted? Will you keep trying to build back the old picture, following directions that don't seem to work anymore? Or you could take all the pieces of your broken life that you can find and put them into the hands of God and watch what He can build?

Our God is not only the One who redeems our lives; He is also a creative God. He made the universe out of what did not exist. God can make something out of nothing. He does not need your picture on the box. He does not need your directions. He does, however, very much need those broken pieces. And the place to start as we look at the end of Naomi and Ruth's story is to pick them all up and put them in His hands, because God has His own picture, and it is amazing!

BROKEN PIECES

Naomi is a woman who knows all about broken pieces. We have watched through the pages of the book of Ruth as her life fell apart, bit by bit. Before the famine, Naomi had one very nice pirate ship. Her family was set—a great husband, two sons, a farm. Every piece in place.

Her pirate ship was safe on a shelf, but then famine came, followed by a trip to Moab. In Moab her life began to come apart, piece by piece, until finally it all came crashing down as she experienced the death of her husband and then the loss of her two sons. Can you just hear the deafening sound as that ship hits the ground, pieces going everywhere, never to be built again? Can you picture the frantic Naomi scurrying around the dirt floor of her small home in Moab, frantically grabbing at stray pieces before they disappear? And all the while she knew there was little hope at all of building life back to the only picture she knew.

We have watched her and listened to her and marveled at her strength as she, together with Ruth, allowed God to build a new life for them back in Bethlehem. As much as Naomi had voiced her strong displeasure as she trudged back home, spitting out words of bitterness and pain, the truth was that as she began to live life anew in her old hometown, she did so with empty, expectant hands. Walking up and down the streets of that familiar city must have brought back memories of a life she once lived and cherished, and throughout that process God received back every single one of the broken pieces of her life. One by one she handed them back to Him. Each time she dropped one into His loving hands, a part of her released the picture she once had loved and admired, the picture she had worked so hard to build, the picture she would never see again.

Years of famine and death had taken that picture away. But new hope had begun to paint a brand new picture, one in which she would not only find a Redeemer; she would learn that what she ended up with was actually better than what she had lost. What could be better than a pirate ship, you ask. What could be better than having your loving husband and sons around you? I will tell you what is better: living life in clear view of God's picture. Living with hands that are empty of broken pieces, with a heart that is recaptured, with eyes that shine with hope, with a brand new grandchild on your lap and a beautiful, loving daughter-in-law that is better than seven sons, that is what. In the midst of all that loss, there is truly a way to love the new picture even more than you did the old one. But that requires giving God all those pieces and keeping your hands wide open for Him to fill them with what He has in mind.

BETTER

We left our gals chatting and giddy over the hope ignited by the long romantic night at the threshing floor. Naomi had assured Ruth that Boaz would do all that was necessary to redeem them, and that is exactly what he did. Boaz met with the leaders of the town, along with the other near relative of Naomi, to decide who would redeem Ruth and Naomi. There, at the city gate, a transaction takes place full of ancient near east tradition.

Boaz is given the opportunity to redeem Ruth, and he wastes no time in doing so. He takes her to be his wife. Everyone in the town celebrates and gives them their blessing. Ruth has a child. That child will be the grandfather of King David, almost exactly in the middle of the line age of the King of Kings, the Redeemer of all mankind, Jesus. That beautiful little child sits on the lap of his beaming grandmother as the ladies of the town gather around her.

These same women had said goodbye to Naomi so many years ago as she left for Moab with her own small sons. These same women had listened to a bitter and hurting Naomi as she returned home from Moab empty. Those women now joyfully celebrate the life of this child, and as they do so, they are careful to note that Naomi is the one who was not left without a Redeemer. True, Ruth is the one who got the guy, but Naomi is the one who was redeemed. Why?

Because she had the most pieces. I am sure it was through tears of joy that she remembered all that had come and gone from her life during years of famine and death. I wonder where her thoughts traveled as she rocked her grandson in the same rhythmic motion she had used with her own boys. Did she think about the old picture she had treasured? Did she hear that familiar, horrific crash as those dreams died, and the pieces of that beloved pirate ship fell to the ground?

But into the painful memories came words of immense and utter truth, words from the mouths of those same women, the standbyers of her life, the ones who observed, the ones who had taken in the pain and loss. The truth was so clear to them. Their words were direct and honest as they said that Ruth had been better to Naomi than any of the sons she had lost. Ruth had loved Naomi enough to not escape or ignore the famine, but to honestly endure it right beside her. She had been determined, even when Naomi had tried to push her away. She had worked, and she had listened and obeyed what Naomi had asked.

And now as Ruth stood by, lovingly watching her mother-in-law rock this child who held so much promise, her satisfaction must have been overwhelming. The picture was so perfect, yet it had come as the result of so much pain and loss. Contrary to normal expectations, such pain and loss do seem to make the most beautiful pictures. It is only when the broken pieces of our lives end up in the hands of the One who made us that we can really begin to see what our life is supposed to look like. So what are you waiting for? How many pieces do you have in your hands? And what is keeping you from handing them to your Redeemer?

HOLDING ONTO THE PIECES

Every once and a while at my house, when we are about to embark on a job none of us likes—for example, weeding our yard—I remind my boys that if it was easy or even fun, we would have already done it. It is the same with many of the broken places in our lives. If it was easy, or even fun, to take those places to God, we would already have done it. But the reality is, most of us hold onto the broken pieces for months, years, sometimes even for a lifetime. We endure the famine.

We have to live with the results of the deaths in our lives, but instead of experiencing those beautiful moments like we just noted in Ruth and Naomi, we never quite see the new picture because we are unwilling to release our old one. We still are looking at that old box top with the picture of our pirate ship, directions in hand, surrounded by thousands of pieces, trying desperately to make them fit. Stop asking the wrong questions. Stop asking why the directions no longer work, and begin asking why you still have those pieces in your hands.

OUR FAILURES

Maybe you don't want to hand those pieces over to Him because you know that some of what is broken in your life is because of you. Maybe you have escaped from a famine or two and ended up in Moab, and you are ashamed. He desperately wants those pieces, too; He wants you to come home. He wants your failures, your mistakes, your bad choices that sent your dreams crashing to the ground. He loves you today; He died for those broken pieces in your hands. He wants you to trust that He is not only your Redeemer but also a Creator, and as Creator God He can make something out of a broken mess. So if you believe that "nothing" good can come out of your life, just hand him that mess and see what He can build. You will be amazed at how beautiful, how useful, how incredibly powerful a life He can build from the broken pieces of your failures.

THE FAILURE OF OTHERS

The other thing that might be keeping you from handing Him the pieces is that they were broken by someone else. You don't want to give them up because somehow to sit there in the broken mess of your life feels like the only thing you can do. You are a victim, and there is a villain out there who broke your dream apart. You are afraid that if you hand those broken pieces over to God, that person will get off easy, and there is something strangely comforting about sitting in that pile of broken pieces. After all, bitterness and anger feel kind of good after awhile, and if nothing else, with those pieces in your hand you will at least have something to throw at them as a reminder of what they took from you.

But you don't have to remain a victim, and that villain you are staring down does not have to stay the size of King Kong. If you stop hurling those pieces for a second and take a look around you, I believe you will not see victims or villains, but instead just a pile of broken pieces and hurting people. The first step toward forgiveness is picking up the pieces and handing them to God, freeing yourself and that person to let God create something new.

The problem is that often we don't want something new. We want the picture on the box, we want our dream. We want our health back, we want the perfect marriage, we want the baby we could never seem to have. We want the life back that others have taken from us. And we want to have all the pieces at our disposal to make that happen. To be brutally honest, we are afraid that if we hand God all the pieces, He won't give us the picture on the box. He will give us something different, and the hard truth is, we don't want it. We want what life is supposed to be like, we want what the directions promised us, we want the picture. So does God, but it's His picture, and we will never see that picture of His when we are gripping those broken pieces in our hands.

It's not Broken

Maybe you do not want to hand Him the pieces because they are not broken. You have been careful, you have followed all the directions, you have all the pieces in place. Your pirate ship is still safely on the shelf and you guard it very carefully. You have known few famines, little death, and no great struggles. Your life looks like the picture, and you love it. Why would you want to give it to God?

I will tell you why: because He has an even better picture.

When our life is not broken, we are really good about saying things like, "I have given everything over to God; oh yes, it all belongs to Him—my life, my finances, my job, my marriage, my kids, my health, it's all His." Is it really? I bet Naomi used to say those words before the famine. I can tell you I said those kinds of words hundreds of times about my life. I told God He had my boys. I said they belonged to Him, never thinking for a moment that He would allow anything to happen that I would not approve of.

What happens when you have given your whole pirate ship to God unbroken and whole and you watch Him begin to mess with the pieces? I don't know about you, but I start to grab that ship back pretty quickly.

"I mean, come on, God, you didn't really think I meant you could play with it."

"Watch out, don't mess with that piece, God, because if you move it that whole section will fall apart!"

Have you ever had that kind of a conversation with God? We don't do it out loud; we do it in our minds, and it's called fear. Nothing that is eternal can ever be built on fear. Let it go, give it up, you can trust Him. He is in control. As great as you think your picture is, as nice as that ship looks up on the shelf, wouldn't you like to get a look at what God's picture is for you?

SOVEREIGN

You don't have to spend a long time with my boys to know they are a bunch of really cool guys. They are not perfect; in fact life has hit them hard, and they have scars to show for it. They have already watched some pretty amazing treasures fall to the ground, and they are not happy about it. As a matter of fact, they have been angry and they have every right to be. If they wanted to, they could be throwing broken pieces all over the place, but instead, they are slowly learning to hand them to God. My boys know the truth that life in this fallen world is broken, and it hurts to be broken. They also know that what is broken can somehow be fixed. It may not look the same, for it looks kind of like real life. At times it is painful and confusing, often deep, always crazy, sometimes as joyful as it is ridiculous. And to the core, life is good.

My sons will be amazing men, each one of them. Does our life look like the picture I always had in my mind? No, it is vastly different, but I love what God has done with the broken pieces. Is it an easy life? No way! Is it good? Oh yes. It is good because it is His picture. He took the broken pieces of divorce and severe disability, and He is creating something new. I don't know how it will turn out. I don't have the cover of the box, and thankfully, I don't have the directions, either. But the most important part is that God has the pieces. He alone knows what it will look like. He is not only our Redeemer, He is not only our Creator and the One who recaptures our hearts; He is also sovereign.

The word "sovereign" used in reference to God is found almost three hundred times in the Bible. A sovereign is defined as one having supreme authority and power, and that is who God is. What that means for us is that He is in control. The amazing part of that control is that He is ruler even over our own choices and the choices of others. He can somehow mold them all, even the lousy, hurtful ones, into the picture He alone knows.

So when the world is crashing around us, when we are in the middle of famine and death, when the pieces are flying all over the place, God still has a plan. He still is in control. God still has a picture in His mind, and the great news is that He is sovereign, which means that He can take the broken pieces of our failures. He can take the hurtful choices of others. He can take the silent dreams of our hearts and create His dream for us. His picture. That picture is amazing; if you don't believe me, just ask Ruth and Naomi. But the key is, He has to have all the pieces.

So what would keep you from giving them to Him today? Is it guilt? Pride? Is it anger, bitterness, or fear? Maybe you have held onto that picture so long that you don't even know if you can pry your fingers off it. Don't you want His dream for you? Don't you want Him to take the broken pieces of your life and make something new? Aren't you curious about what it will look like? Don't you want to start living it? Aren't you sick of staying in that pile of broken parts, staring at a dream that is impossible for you to rebuild?

I would guess that if you are sitting right now in a pile of broken dreams, you are probably sitting there alone. We are usually left alone in our pain when our dreams die. But I can promise you something today: in God's dream you are not alone. His picture of your life contains people you have never even met. You have no way of knowing how big His dream is for you; nor do you have any idea of the people you will touch when you turn the broken pieces of your life over to Him.

HIS PICTURE INCLUDES OTHERS

I will never forget the afternoon when I was asked to speak in the high security section of a women's prison in Almaty, Kazakhstan. It was a work prison with over 1,500 inmates. This particular section held the women who were the most dangerous, some because they had just arrived and others because they would never leave.

We entered the grounds of this prison within a prison called La Culka. There were high walls with barbed wire around the top of them. When we entered with the staff of chaplains and guards, the women would not look up and make eye contact. But they kept coming, and by the time our meeting started in their damp, dark cafeteria, the room was full. They looked so similar to each other. All wore scarves over their tanned, weathered skin. As they filed in, they had their faces to the ground.

They were silent until the Chaplain welcomed them and began to sing. Then, suddenly the room was filled with energy as the women lifted their voices to God. Their eyes filled with tears, their hands were raised in the air that was now filled with worship. As we spoke to them that day it was like drops of water in a desert; they literally absorbed every single word. I knew that these dear ladies, these women, who much like Naomi had known great loss, these women who had watched their dreams fall on the ground and break before their eyes, these women were part of God's picture for my life.

That day they did not need to hear from a woman who looked like the picture from the box cover. They did not need to hear from someone who had all the pieces and knew how they fit. No, those precious women needed to hear from a single mom who was raising her four sons. They needed to hear from the broken heart of a mother who raised a son who would always be two years old, no matter how big and strong he got. They needed to hear what it felt like, what it looked like, and what it sounded like when her dreams came crashing down. And most of all they needed to know that there was a God big enough to hold all those broken pieces. They needed to know that they could be redeemed. They needed to know that, even in the middle of a dry work camp, God still loved them. God could use even their famine and the death of their hopes and dreams to recapture their hearts.

JOSEPH

There was someone else who sat in a lonely prison cell who could have told those women the very same thing. He would have told them God could not only reach down and redeem their lives; He would help them through this famine. And most of all, he would tell them that what they learn as they endure the famine and live in the midst of loss will save the lives of others.

That man's name was Joseph. Joseph was the favored son of Jacob. You are likely aware of his story found at the end of the book of Genesis. His ten brothers hated him for the attention he got from his father, and that hate overflowed to the point of violence. They plotted to sell their brother into slavery. They beat him up, threw him into a pit, and waited for a caravan headed to Egypt to take him along. The brothers then told their heartbroken father that Joseph had been killed, and Joseph himself was left to live a new and dark life on his own. Talk about a broken pirate ship! As it fell to the ground, Joseph's loss must have felt and sounded more like the wreck of a luxury cruise vessel than that of a mere pirate ship.

Instead of sitting in a pile of broken pieces, Joseph handed them all to God. He had to do that not only once, but several times throughout his young life. First, he was falsely accused by the wife of his owner and sent to prison. Crash! Then, while in prison he helped interpret dreams for several men who promised to get him out when they were freed, but they promptly forgot. Another blow! Another chance to hand God broken pieces.

Finally, after all these hurts and disappointments he was given an opportunity to interpret the dream of the Pharaoh himself, an achievement that freed him not only from prison, but vaulted him to the second highest position in all of Egypt. During his tenure as a leader, Joseph took the knowledge he interpreted from the dream and built a commerce system around it, thus saving up food and supplies for an upcoming famine.

When the famine finally hit, Joseph was able to feed much of the known world, saving millions, including his own family. His ability to endure the famine allowed him to share with many others what he had learned in the midst of that struggle, thus literally saving their lives. Each and every one of those people he saved was in God's picture for Joseph's life. I am sure that in the pit and in the prison he had no idea what that picture looked like. All he could see was broken pieces, and all he could do was gather them all up and hand them to his God. His Redeemer took care of the rest.

GOD'S PICTURE

Recaptured hearts, redeemed lives, death, famine, hope, and a harvest. We have looked at many things together through the timeless pages of the book of Ruth. But this book is not about Ruth or Naomi. It is not about my life or the lives of my sons, it is not about the countless other lives we have looked at. No, this book is about you. It's about your heart and your Redeemer who has given everything up to recapture it. He wants to come to where you are; He wants to live right beside you.

He wants to come to you in the dry and desolate fields of your life and whisper words of hope. He wants to sit beside you on the deck of the pool when pain and grief have caused you to be stuck there. He wants to walk beside you on the long journey home. He wants to hear the tearful, angry, bitter cries of your heart as you watch death steal your hopes, your dreams, someone you loved, or the loss of a love you would never know. He has been there, and He is waiting still. Will you go to Him, will you approach your Redeemer? Will you come with your hands full of broken pieces and leave them at His feet?

You will see His picture someday. It will not be on a box top; it will be painted across the canvas of heaven. Someday you, all alone, completely by yourself, will stand and face your Redeemer. Will you have a trash bag full of the broken pieces of your life? Will you dump it out in front of Him and recount every famine, every moment of pain and loss to Him? Will you look up at Him with eyes filled with bitterness and anger and spit out the words, "Where were You when all this came crashing down? Didn't You know how much this would all hurt?"

In response, He will gather the broken pieces of your life, and with disappointment and despair in His eyes He will tell you that He was right beside you. He will point to the picture He had painted of your life, the one He had been looking at all those years, and He will simply say that He needed those pieces to build it. He might point to Naomi's picture and tell you how she had given them all to Him, and just look what He built for her. Look at the picture of her life! She was not left without a Redeemer. She did not wait until heaven to voice her complaint, to hand over the brokenness of her life. She did it while alive, and because of that, she really lived out God's picture.

Maybe when you reach heaven you will still be carrying that pirate ship intact. You will set it down in front of him with sureness as you wait for his approval, but you will not hear the words, "Well done."[2] Instead your Redeemer will point to His picture and tell you He needed that boat. He needed every part to build His picture. It is not enough to live out life the way you want to; you must live life the way it is. You cannot escape the famines; nor can you protect yourself or the ones you love from them. It takes a lot of energy to keep that boat on the shelf. Every bit of that energy is directed right back at you. There is no more selfish a life than one lived with the sole purpose of keeping your life from crashing to the ground. That is not how you want to see your picture. You do not want to look up from your perfect little life and see the full and abundant one He had planned for you.

No, what you really want is to walk into His presence and fall at His feet with empty hands. Like Ruth, you can turn and look with Him at the picture of your life. You can share every detail together because you lived it all. You met all those people He had in mind. You shared what you had learned with them. You know all about the picture; you have seen it a million times as you lay at the feet of your Redeemer. And yes, He will use that beautiful masterpiece, that picture of your life. Yes, He will use even *that* to recapture your heart—for all of eternity.

Endnotes

Introduction

1. Matthew 15:22
2. Matthew 15:24
3. Ezekiel 14:5

Chapter 1

1. Ruth 1:1-2
2. Judges 17:6
3. Isaiah 50:7
4. Acts 3:2
5. 2 Chronicles 20:12
6. 1 Kings 17:1
7. Psalm 46:10
8. 1 Kings 17:9
9. Matthew 26:42
10. Ezekiel 14:5

Chapter 2

1. Ruth 1:3-5
2. Matthew 17:20

3. Hebrews 11:1
4. Exodus 16:22
5. Exodus 16:27
6. John 6:48
7. Ephesians 1:13
8. John 3:16
9. 1 Samuel 1:11
10. 1 Samuel 1:24-28
11. 1 Samuel 2:6
12. John 11:23
13. John 11:25

Chapter 3

1. Ruth 1:6-13
2. Genesis 12:1-3
3. Genesis 18:14
4. Genesis 21:6
5. Genesis 18:14
6. Romans 8:37-39
7. www.fragilehearts.org

Chapter 4

1. Ruth 1:14-18
2. Ruth 1:15
3. Genesis 12:3
4. Genesis 15:13-14
5. Ruth 1:16-17
6. Deuteronomy 30:19
7. 1 John 1:9
8. Hebrews 3:6, 3:14, 4:14, 6:18, 10:23
9. Hebrews 10:22 The Message
10. 1 Corinthians 2:16
11. Amos 4:13
12. 2 Corinthians 10:5
13. Philippians 4:8

14. Ephesians 4:29
15. Isaiah 41:10

Chapter 5

1. Ruth 1:19-22
2. Matthew 4:1-11
3. Ruth 1:20-21
4. Job 2:10
5. Job 42:5
6. Job 42:7-8
7. Hebrews 11:17
8. Genesis 1-2
9. Hebrews 11:3
10. Revelation 21:5
11. Lamentations 3:22-23
12. Zephaniah 3:20

Chapter 6

1. Ruth 2
2. Isaiah 25:1
3. Joshua 2:8-12
4. Ruth 2:12
5. Hebrews 6:19
6. Joshua 17:18
7. Ruth 2:12
8. Hebrews 11:24-27
9. Hebrews 11:13-16

Chapter 7

1. Ruth 3
2. Galatians 5:1
3. C. Austin Miles, In the Garden, March, 1912
4. Philippians 2:8
5. Joshua 10:12

Chapter 8

1. Ruth 4
2. Matthew 25:23

CPSIA information can be obtained
at www.ICGtesting.com
Printed in the USA
FSOW02n0747140715
8832FS